Praise for *Empowered YOUth*

"*Michael and Jeffrey Eisen deliver a powerful message that shows us that we do not have to wait one more minute to step into an inspired life. With touching stories, we are reminded of the importance of deep, intimate relationships, understanding how our minds work, and having the courage to be who we truly are. This book just may inspire a generation of Americans to get involved, bring their talents to public service, and help steer America in an exciting new direction that can help us recapture the American spirit!*"

— **Congressman Tim Ryan**, author of *A Mindful Nation*

"*Michael and Jeffrey offer a powerful blueprint of how parents and children can truly befriend each other so as to grow, heal, and flourish in life. I recommend their work wholeheartedly.*"

— **Robert Holden, Ph.D.,** author of *Shift Happens!*

"***Empowered YOUth** is a transformative book written by a wise and loving father-and-son team. Through their engaging journey, Jeffrey and Michael help deconstruct the paradigms and beliefs that contribute to family stress, anxiety, and unrest. They provide a refreshing perspective on how parents and youth can work together to encourage and support one another by opening the channels of communication, surrendering the need for control, and leading by shining example. This book has the power to strengthen families for generations to come.*"

— **Kris Carr**, *New York Times* best-selling author of *Crazy Sexy Diet*

"*The compassionate wisdom shared by Jeffrey and Michael Eisen in* **Empowered YOUth** *is exactly what the world needs right now. Read it with an open mind . . . but live it with an open heart. Michael and Jeffrey's inspiring journey shows the importance of cultivating a life of awareness and tapping into the power of self-love. By reading this book, you will discover a pathway to healing your life, your chil* . . . . . . *our planet.*"

— **Michael J. Chase**, founder of The K . . . *n I being kind: how asking one simple question* . . . *world*

"***Empowered YOUth** is an incredibly* . . . *ractical tools and strategies to help you live a happier, healthier, ... ered life. Whether you are young or old, a parent or a teenager, a teacher or a student, or someone who simply cares for the well-being of youth in our society, this book will inspire you to create positive change in your life and the lives of others.*"

— **Mike Robbins**, author of *Be Yourself: Everyone Else Is Already Taken*

"Michael and Jeffrey Eisen, a father-son team who struggled with their relationship for many years, provide hope for all parents and children who long to not only heal from past wounds, but also to use the healing journey as an opportunity for transcendence. With practical wisdom and insight, they give us both inspiration and tools for how to transform past traumas and troubled relationships into fuel for stoking the fires of a more empowered and conscious life. **Empowered YOUth** provides a road map for how to heal old wounds, repair past conflicts, alchemize life's pains into gold, and flourish with a new perspective on love, the pursuit of happiness, and the meaning of life. It's a must read for every parent or child who yearns for reconciliation and longs to awaken."

— **Lissa Rankin, M.D.**, author, founder of **OwningPink.com**, and blogger at **LissaRankin.com**

"Wouldn't all of our lives be better if we understood our parents and our parents understood us? The journey of understanding between father (Jeffrey) and son (Michael) in **Empowered YOUth**, and their coming together for a common purpose, breathes new life into the struggles of all ages. Through their stories and process, they teach us all the principles of conscious living, and how passing these on to our children can create a ripple effect for generations to come."

— **Michelle Phillips,** best-selling author of *The Beauty Blueprint: 8 Steps to Building the Life and Look of Your Dreams*

"**Empowered YOUth** awakens our consciousness so that we can become positive guides for the next generation. If we want a healthier, happier, more abundant future, we must shift our own energy and inspire the next generation to follow suit. **Empowered YOUth** is our guide to changing the world one mindful thought at a time."

— **Gabrielle Bernstein**, best-selling author of *Spirit Junkie*

"Throughout history, the father-son relationship has been known to be notoriously rocky, often expressed with a lack of communication, rivalries, or simple misunderstandings. Jeffrey and Michael Eisen look to change all that with their inspiring story in **Empowered YOUth**. A heartfelt, down-to-earth, and highly applicable book, and a must read for not just fathers and sons, but all parents, children, and anyone who wants a deeper understanding of the parent-child bond and how to bring that relationship to its highest possibilities."

— **Nick Ortner**, executive producer, *The Tapping Solution*

"Michael and Jeffrey Eisen close the so-called generation gap, proving that the human connection and spirit are ageless. As a parent, I was inspired by this story of how a father and son went from divided to united through transformational work, reinventing their family, and creating a template for those of us who want to experience love, not struggle, in all our closest relationships. With young people facing greater challenges than ever, this work is a timely must read to consciously raise the next generation.

— **Ophira Edut**, The AstroTwins (**www.astrostyle.com**), author of *Body Outlaws*, and founder of **www.loveyourbody.org**

emPOWERed
YOUth

Hay House Titles of Related Interest

YOU CAN HEAL YOUR LIFE, the movie,
starring Louise L. Hay & Friends
(available as a 1-DVD program and an expanded 2-DVD set)
Watch the trailer at: **www.LouiseHayMovie.com**

THE SHIFT, the movie,
starring Dr. Wayne W. Dyer
(available as a 1-DVD program and an expanded 2-DVD set)
Watch the trailer at: **www.DyerMovie.com**

▦ ▣ ▨

THE ART OF EXTREME SELF-CARE:
Transform Your Life One Month at a Time, by Cheryl Richardson

THE INTUITIVE SPARK: Bringing Intuition Home to Your Child, Your
Family, and You, by Sonia Choquette

THE SAINT, THE SURFER, AND THE CEO: A Remarkable Story
about Living Your Heart's Desires, by Robin Sharma

SECRETS OF MEDITATION: A Practical Guide to Inner Peace
and Transformation, by davidji

WISHES FULFILLED: Mastering the Art of Manifesting,
by Dr. Wayne W. Dyer

All of the above are available at your local bookstore,
or may be ordered by visiting:

Hay House USA: **www.hayhouse.com**®
Hay House Australia: **www.hayhouse.com.au**
Hay House UK: **www.hayhouse.co.uk**
Hay House South Africa: **www.hayhouse.co.za**
Hay House India: **www.hayhouse.co.in**

emPOWERed YOUth

A Father and Son's Journey to Conscious Living

Michael Eisen and Jeffrey Eisen

HAY HOUSE, INC.
Carlsbad, California • New York City
London • Sydney • Johannesburg
Vancouver • Hong Kong • New Delhi

Published and distributed in the United States by: Hay House, Inc.: www.hay house.com® • *Published and distributed in Australia by:* Hay House Australia Pty. Ltd.: www.hayhouse.com.au • *Published and distributed in the United Kingdom by:* Hay House UK, Ltd.: www.hayhouse.co.uk • *Published and distributed in the Republic of South Africa by:* Hay House SA (Pty), Ltd.: www.hayhouse.co.za • *Distributed in Canada by:* Raincoast: www.raincoast.com • *Published in India by:* Hay House Publishers India: www.hayhouse.co.in

Editor: Hailey Eisen
Cover design: Amy Rose Grigoriou • *Interior design:* Pamela Homan

Library of Congress Cataloging-in-Publication Data

Eisen, Michael.
  Empowered youth : a father and son's journey to conscious living / Michael Eisen, Jeffrey Eisen.
    p. cm.
  ISBN 978-1-4019-3938-0 (tradepaper : alk. paper) -- ISBN 978-1-4019-3940-3 (ebook)
  1. Fathers and sons. 2. Interpersonal relations. I. Eisen, Jeffrey. II. Title.
  HQ755.85.E394 2012
  306.874'2--dc23
                          2012021734

Tradepaper ISBN: 978-1-4019-3938-0
Digital ISBN: 978-1-4019-3940-3

15 14 13 12   4 3 2 1
1st edition, October 2012

Printed in the United States of America

To Lois Eisen
for keeping the love alive in our family,
even during difficult times;

to Louise Hay for
believing in us and the importance of
empowering young people;

and to the youth of today and tomorrow,
who hold the power to change
the world for the better.

CONTENTS

FOREWORD

I believe that affirmations are for everyone, from tiny babies to people who are just leaving the planet. The earlier we can learn how to think and how to speak in a more positive and supportive way, the fewer problems we will create in our lives.

Up until now, most of the self-empowerment books that have been written have been for grown-ups. But grown-ups aren't the only ones who have issues—young people have challenges with life, too. For a long time, I have wanted to address this and bring the message to young adults, teenagers, and children. I want them to know that every thought we think and every word we speak is an affirmation about ourselves and about life. Instead of tearing ourselves down, we want to build ourselves up.

Yet I am aware that I am not the person to actually deliver the message, because young people need to speak to young people. I wondered where I could find the perfect individual who already had this understanding, and through whom I could then further pass down my knowledge to be shared with this younger audience.

Then one day, Life said, "All right, we're here to help you." I was introduced to the charming Michael Eisen, who was already working with young people. Our connection was instantaneous—both our visions and messages were perfectly aligned and flowed beautifully together. Michael has now become one of my favorite students. I know that everything he learns from me, and his own life experience, will be shared with the next generation.

Michael and his father, Jeffrey, have written this wonderful new book, *Empowered YOUth*. There are many books written by mothers and daughters, but I believe this is one of the first written by a father and son. The information they share on how we can heal old entrenched issues is so useful for *all* families. It provides insight on how each member can express his or her own unique perspective on everything, and be able to do so in a safe and comfortable environment. It inspires and empowers everyone to be the best and most authentic version of themselves. It provides simple strategies for how children can grow up acknowledging their own worth, increasing their own self-esteem, and feeling safe and supported by Life itself.

There is a better life to be lived if we are willing to make some changes in the way we think, speak, and act. Parents can heal, children can heal, and entire families can heal together; Michael and Jeffrey show us a way.

I believe *Empowered YOUth* will have a big positive impact and create many profound changes in the lives of parents, families, children, teachers, students, and anyone who is in close contact with a child. I love this book, and I am sure you will enjoy it, too.

— **Louise Hay**

INTRODUCTION

When I first met with Reid Tracy, president and CEO of Hay House, and Louise Hay in a meeting room at the Toronto Convention Centre in May 2011, my hope was to share with them my passion for empowering and inspiring youth, and to determine how I might be able to get Hay House involved in my recently founded organization, the Youth Wellness Network. I was just a 25-year-old recent college graduate, trying to live out the dream of making a difference in the world. But there I was, sitting next to these two incredibly influential and accomplished people—and if I told you I wasn't freaking out just a bit, I'd be lying. Truthfully, the idea of writing a book for Hay House hadn't even crossed my mind at the time, and I was over the moon just to have a few uninterrupted minutes with these two amazing individuals. I took a deep breath and shared with them the story of my life:

> *I was a small-town kid who struggled in most social situations and spent the majority of my childhood fighting with my parents, pissing off my siblings, struggling to fit in with my peers, and unsuccessfully trying to conform to the standards society had set. I was not a happy kid, and I rarely felt comfortable in my own skin. In my desperate quest for freedom, I came off as angry and ungrateful, while leaving a lot of harsh feelings in my wake.*
>
> *My dad, on the other hand, came across as an extremely confident and overly accomplished man who had it all figured*

out and was on the fast-track to success. He appeared to be always in control and valued that control more than anything else. He liked things his way, had well laid-out expectations for his kids, and didn't have much patience for my antics. Business was his priority, and family appeared to come second. Needless to say, we rarely saw eye to eye and didn't have much of a relationship.

When I finally left for university, I was eager for a fresh start. While I overcame my issues of awkwardness and really started to work the social scene, I still struggled with self-confidence and was desperately searching for freedom. I couldn't seem to find a balance between partying and studying, and as a result spent most of my time feeling torn, out of place, and stressed out. While I was counting on the four years of college to be the best years of my life, it turned out that all the pressure I heaped upon myself eventually led to a breakdown. And while I was away, experiencing "freedom" and realizing it wasn't all it was cracked up to be, my dad was at home going through what some would call a midlife crisis.

For the first 19 years of my life and the first 50 years of my dad's, neither of us were truly who we appeared to be. We had, like many, been inundated with beliefs, values, and standards set by others that we struggled to keep up with and make our own. Neither of us was particularly happy—but we didn't realize it at the time.

When my dad entered his sixth decade, he found himself in a hospital bed reevaluating everything. Discontentment and dissatisfaction had finally caught up with him, and he knew he could no longer go on the way he had been. He had huge decisions to make about what he'd do with his business, where he would go, and how he would experience the next part of his life. Thus began his journey of self-discovery, which, ten years later, has totally changed his life in the best ways possible.

The timing of this couldn't have been any better—for me, anyway—because just as I was feeling the bottom fall out of my world, my dad was starting up a practice as a life coach.

As fate would have it, I became one of his first students; and through months of learning and reprogramming, our relationship transformed from one of resentment to one of love and mutual admiration.

If it weren't for my dad, I don't know where I'd be today. Thanks to his courage to take a leap and start over, I was able to follow in his footsteps and re-create my own life. Today, we couldn't be happier, and sometimes it's hard for our family and friends to believe that we are the same two people who struggled so much for all those years.

My dad now runs a successful coaching practice out of his home in Toronto and has helped hundreds of people begin and progress on their own personal journeys of self-discovery. He has found his purpose in awakening, empowering, and inspiring others by sharing his love and wisdom. He has surrendered all need for control and, as a result, has a much more peaceful and enjoyable life.

I, too, am living my passion. I run my own business, the Youth Wellness Network, with the mandate of empowering youth across the globe to live happier and more positive lives. I now speak to, and provide wellness programs and resources for, thousands of young people every year. While I did face challenges as I struggled to break free from traditional expectations and trust in my own ability to define success, today I am living on my own terms.

Who knew that after sharing my life story with Louise and Reid, they'd not only be impressed and eager to get involved with my mission to empower young people, but also see a great idea for a book. They wanted my dad and me to tell our story together, reaching out with the message that no relationship is beyond repair, and that parents and kids can come together to not only exist harmoniously, but also to inspire change in each other.

And so we set out to write this book, spending ten months digging up old memories, forgiving past transgressions, and observing the similarities in our stories as we each worked to recount how we got to where we are at today. Our family became involved in the process: my sister working as our editor and my mom as our proofreader. The memories had different effects on all of us, but I can truthfully say that this opportunity has been successful in bringing us closer as we learned to let go of the past.

This book isn't just our life stories, but more important, a collection of the most important lessons, insights, and principles that influenced and supported our journey to conscious living. Through these teachings, we believe you will come to realize that everyone has the ability to change his or her life for the better. When you believe in yourself and are committed, anything is possible. We hope you will relate to our story in some way, take in the lessons we share and make them your own, and feel inspired enough to begin your own journey to live the Empowered YOU!

— **Michael Eisen**

A FEW WORDS ABOUT
THIS BOOK

This book is both an autobiographical recount of each of our experiences as we navigated our way through life and a series of lessons and teachings we uncovered and adopted along the way. Each of our stories was written independently, and any similarities or patterns in how we related the events are purely coincidental.

As we each progress on our journey and become more self-confident and self-aware, you will find that our stories move from struggle to awakening, from conflict to cooperation, from control to freedom, and from fear to love. While our experiences may seem somewhat typical at times, what we hope you'll learn from us is that no matter what life deals you, you always have the choice to seek out something better and more meaningful. Although we were more than three decades apart, we each had childhoods filled with stress, sadness, loneliness, and despair. While we both had what others would consider good upbringings, we felt extremely uncomfortable and unsettled during this time. No matter what a person's life looks like from the outside, it's what he's feeling on the inside that creates his reality.

We know that many of you are facing similar struggles, and we hope that in sharing our stories we'll be able to inspire you to find the courage to make the changes necessary to shift from despair to empowerment.

Throughout this book, we share our principles of conscious living—the insights, philosophies, and truths that serve as the foundation for how we live. You will find these mixed in with our stories and highlighted in learning boxes and sidebars. While some of these principles may be dramatically different from what you've been taught up to now, we ask that you come at them with an open mind and an open heart. Some changes will happen quickly, and others will take time. This is not a race, nor a competition. If something doesn't resonate with you, feel free to leave it and move on.

At the end of the book you will find the Resources section, which we hope will help you turn learning into doing and, eventually, habit. This section includes exercises, activities, and practices that you can make part of your daily routine or pull out when you're in a pinch. These are just a handful of the many techniques that have helped us to implement the principles of conscious living— many of which we continue to use today. Feel free to pick and choose what works for you, and please remember to come back to this section often, whenever you're in need of some assistance.

By taking the time to read this book, we hope you will be able to learn more about your true self and understand others better. We believe that your relationships will improve, and the things you want will begin to flow in great abundance. Once you begin to lead an empowered and conscious life, you'll be able to empower the next generation to do the same. As parents and kids, teachers and students, mentors and mentees, we can bridge the gap between generations and come together to create a new future that is full of compassion, understanding, empowerment, and true happiness for everyone!

Chapter One

IN THE BEGINNING . . .

Jeffrey's Story

I was born on May 28, 1952, in Pembroke, a rural lumber town in Eastern Ontario, nestled on the bank of the Ottawa River. My father owned and operated a scrap-metal business, and my mother managed the home. I was the second born and would soon come to take my place as the middle child, with a social butterfly for an older sister and a jock for a little brother. I wasn't into sports and I didn't have many friends, so I could have been identified as a geek thanks to the oversized glasses that were perched upon my nose and the two silver caps that replaced my front teeth. Even as a young boy, I didn't feel particularly comfortable in my own skin. Looking back, I can say with certainty that for most of my childhood I wasn't happy, although I didn't suffer any great injustices. I came from a fairly well-to-do family; my father worked hard to provide for us, and my mother did her best to raise us as she saw fit. I was a product of the 1950s, subject to the rigid social expectations of how a child was supposed to behave.

Now don't get me wrong—I'm not saying that what I went through was more difficult or worse than anyone else's experience. I truly believe that no matter what your circumstances are, it's not about the degree of suffering or disappointment you face, but rather how you feel about life as you're going through it that really matters. And I didn't feel very good.

My earliest vivid memory of childhood takes place on the first day of kindergarten. I was terrified about starting school, as many kids that age are. But instead of crying and clinging to my mother for support, my insides got the better of me and I threw up—all over the classroom floor. So there I was, only five years old and already feeling out of place, foolish, and embarrassed.

That was me: the awkward kid who you'd probably feel sorry for, if you even noticed him at all. I was ill at ease, extremely shy, and totally lacking self-confidence. Like that first day of kindergarten, I struggled through every stage of my youth, and no matter how hard I tried, I never really fit in. Most of my memories are a bit fuzzy—likely because I've forced them out in hopes of forgetting this traumatic time. While I can't recall specific details, thinking about my childhood does bring up an extremely visceral set of emotions, primarily sadness. I was misunderstood, frustrated, lonely, unappreciated, worried, confused, self-conscious, nervous, and unloved. And this was all before I turned ten.

Sadly, the media today is filled with so many stories of young people who are bullied, targeted with hateful acts, and even tempted to commit suicide before they graduate high school. The truth is, if these kids hadn't been beaten down and broken by societal and parental expectations, they'd most likely still be as happy, carefree, and self-loving as they were the day they were born. After all, babies come into the world knowing that they're special, worthy, and loved. So what happens to those happy, carefree, self-loving toddlers that turns them into self-conscious, self-critical children? If our self-worth is truly about how we view and value ourselves, then why do we give so much attention to what others think? Why was I, at five years old, already worried about the impression I'd made on the first day of kindergarten? This isn't something kids are supposed to be tormented about.

As a teenager, I clearly remember crying myself to sleep, wishing I were dead. I'd think: *Why can't I be more like other kids? I just want to fit in. No one understands me. What's the point?* My struggles seemed to intensify the older I got. I was taught that you had to be smart to get ahead, so I made it my mission to excel in school. This only brought on more teasing and ridicule. I not only looked the part of the geek, I acted it, too. Luckily, because I believed so strongly in the power of being smart, I was able to rise above the mean comments and keep my head in my books. But no matter how well I did in school, I didn't actually believe in my own abilities or intellect. Since my self-esteem was shattered, I thought that my good grades were only a result of my hard work, nothing more. I wanted to be successful in life, and the road to success was hard work. That's what my father taught me, and that's what he practiced in his own life, so I dutifully followed suit.

Unlike my brother and sister, I wasn't part of the "in crowd." I felt self-conscious around other kids, and most of the time I kept to myself. I was taught that the way you look is a reflection of who you are. I had a brush cut, wore glasses, had noticeable acne . . . and those two silver caps on my teeth didn't help either. You can only imagine how hard it was for me to look at myself in the mirror. *How can I feel good about myself when I am filled with flaws? Who would want to be friends with someone like me? Try really hard to like what the other kids like and maybe you'll actually fit in,* I'd think. But no matter how hard I tried, I remained a loner and never felt truly happy. I adopted the idea that this was all I could expect out of life.

The beliefs that I was brought up with formed the basis of my thinking as a young person. That's because the foundation for most of what we hold true is created in childhood, especially the early years. When we're young, our brains are like sponges, and we absorb information about everything we see, hear, taste, smell, and touch. For example, if an experience is repeated many times, the belief associated with it eventually becomes our own.

In my case, I absorbed everything my parents and society taught me to be true, and I accepted it all without ever second-guessing its validity. The opinions I held at this stage in my life sounded something like this: *You have to work hard to get ahead. You must be organized, neat, and tidy. You definitely need to be smart. You should be popular or you will be very lonely. You don't really want to stand out from the crowd, unless it's because you're more popular than others. Heaven forbid you should stand out because you're a geek.*

Many of our root beliefs are developed before we have the mental capacity or intellect to discern for ourselves. It's understandable that at a young age we believe that those with more experience and knowledge must know better than we do. In a way, we trust our parents, siblings, and teachers more than we trust ourselves; therefore, we take what they say to be the truth. Around the same time, we're typically being bombarded with so many other messages from peers, the media, religion, and so on that the truth becomes much more obscure. Confusion typically sets in when we're old enough to think for ourselves and realize that some of what we were taught no longer feels right. But as a teen, I wasn't there yet.

My desire to be loved, recognized, and appreciated by my parents was also a tremendous driving force in my life. Around the age of 12, I started working for my father's business at the time, a scrap-metal plant that he and his brother had founded after the Second World War, when they moved to Pembroke from Toronto. I desperately wanted my father's approval, and this was the most direct path to getting it. I can still vividly remember nursing the raw blisters on my hands that formed while sweeping the gigantic paved parking area in front of the scrap yard. This was my first real job, and it gave me a lot of time to think. I was sure that, no matter what, I didn't want to end up doing this for the rest of my life. I hated having sore hands, and decided then and there that I would use my mind to succeed in life, rather than relying on my body for physical labor. My father didn't believe in overpaying me, so I quickly learned how hard I had to work to earn a dollar. While grueling at times, I credit this experience with helping me develop the strong sense of discipline that I relied upon heavily throughout my working life.

In being a part of the family business, even if I was just sweeping, I finally got my father to notice me. So no matter how much I didn't like the job, I kept at it, desperate to make him proud. It was my dad who taught me the value of a strong work ethic, and this has served me well throughout my life. But what came with this discipline was an insatiable determination and desire to drive ahead no matter the cost. I was a total perfectionist. I truly believed that the better I was, the more he and others would pay attention to me. At the time, I was unaware of how much stress and anxiety would accompany these expectations, which I continued to heap upon myself. I didn't realize until many years later how badly I yearned for my father's attention, recognition, and love, and to what ends I would go in order to get it.

Dad likely had no idea that this was even going on. How can a father who isn't feeling good about himself teach a young person to love himself unconditionally and believe in himself completely? He had shown me, without realizing what he was doing, to look up to him, respect and obey him, and seek his approval, just as my grandfather had most likely taught him. And so the cycle continued: he didn't feel good enough about himself, so he demanded the respect of others in an attempt to boost his own self-confidence. But in worshipping him so unwaveringly, I lost my own sense of self and took approval and validation from anyone who would give it to me. This cycle, which exists between many parents and their children, would only be broken years later when I learned to tap into that self-worth I had as a baby and realized that no one except me could provide that feeling of acceptance.

No matter how little I believed in myself, I did a great job of hiding this fact from others. How could I admit to not being good enough? I had to keep my diminished sense of self a secret, outwardly pretending everything was okay. Little did I know that this was literally eating away at my insides. By my mid-teens, after spending many late nights sitting up in our living room suffering from excruciating stomach pains, I was diagnosed with a duodenal ulcer. In short, the stress, nervousness, and anxiety I dealt with on a daily basis had contributed to eating a hole in the wall of my small intestine.

The treatment for ulcers back then was very different than it is today. At the time, they believed it was excess hydrochloric acid in the stomach that caused the ulcer, and, as a result, they had me taking antacids, eating often, and drinking lots of milk in order to neutralize the acidity. I'll never forget hovering around my locker in high school, praying no one would notice as I drank milk from my thermos, ate digestive cookies, and gulped down chalky white antacid medication. This regimen—repeated a few times a day—made it even harder for me to fit in with the other kids my age. And this was only the beginning of my gastrointestinal issues, which I believe were all related to my inability to express my feelings or deal with my emotions. All that pent-up anger, sadness, and fear really took its toll on my system.

In contrast, one of the results of spending so much time at my father's scrap yard was that I got the chance to really know and love my uncle Harry, my father's older brother and business partner. He was a jovial man who was always fun to be around. While still performing the more menial jobs like sweeping, I also spent Saturday mornings working as the office clerk. While my father was out in the plant, my uncle and I would have some interesting discussions inside the office. He became like a second dad to me, showing me all kinds of attention. His own kids were much younger, so I think he also enjoyed our weekly conversations.

While my uncle was an extremely fun-loving person, he did not take care of himself physically. He smoked and ate way too much, didn't watch his weight, and rarely exercised. He was only 46 years old, but those bad habits had already taken their toll. In 1968, Harry suffered a massive heart attack and passed away suddenly. His death left me devastated. I was just 16, I had never experienced death before, and I had no idea how to cope with the feelings of losing him. Although I desperately wanted to cry, I was under the impression that boys were supposed to be tough in circumstances like these and not show their emotions. I took cues from my father, and I held back my tears and tried to be as stoic as I could, knowing that I was really going to miss our times together. His passing was a very traumatic event, but I was not aware until much later how much of an effect it would have on me. This was when I began truly shutting down. It hurt too much to lose someone I loved, so in order to prevent myself from experiencing such pain again, I unconsciously resolved to stop feeling.

Emotions = Energy in Motion

What I was doing as a teenager without really realizing it was trying to control my feelings by avoiding the unpleasant ones and engaging only in the pleasant ones. By doing so, I was cutting myself off from the natural flow of what emotions really are: energy in motion. In essence, they are the free flow of energy that is triggered by our response to what's going on around us. I believe that everything in this world is made up of energy—even humans. So when our vibrating frequency comes in contact with the forces around us, there's a reaction. I'm sure you've experienced this, even if you weren't aware of what was happening. Have you ever noticed that when a really happy individual walks into a room, the whole space seems to light up? But when an angry or stressed-out person enters the same room, it's as if the light is extinguished. That's energy!

If emotions are energy in motion, then when we try to control this force by holding them back, we stop their natural flow and throw ourselves out of balance. Every emotion has a path of movement. In its natural form, it will flow in and through our bodies with relative ease, as long as nothing is blocking its way. Most emotions are allowed to pass through us rather quickly. We can see this in children: because they have not yet been conditioned to judge or stop what they're feeling, babies and young children will go from hysterical tears to giddy glee in a matter of seconds. With no resistance, the energy flows and the emotions are expressed and let go.

As we grow older, we begin to judge and analyze whatever we're feeling. Many of us are taught that expressing ourselves too much is bad, weak, or irresponsible. If we don't have our emotions under control, we're viewed as social outcasts. If we cry in public, it's considered embarrassing. Even someone laughing really loudly oftentimes attracts a lot of unwanted attention. It is these very beliefs that create the misconceptions and misunderstanding around emotions. We are taught to *suppress* instead of *express*.

Sadness and anger are considered "bad" emotions that cause pain and suffering, while joy and pleasure are considered "good" ones that create happiness and bliss. Does this sound familiar? I was taught to believe that feelings are irrational, and if I didn't control them, they'd explode and cause pain to myself and others. Ironically, I experienced so much pain despite doing everything I could to control myself.

When was the last time you stifled the urge to cry, pushed your feelings back down inside, wiped your eyes to hide your tears, or forced yourself to move on with your day? When was the last time that you got so angry your head began to hurt and your stomach tensed up, yet you didn't allow yourself to express this anger or release it? When was the last time you walked into a party and felt so excited that you wanted to squeal and dance around, but you controlled yourself for fear of looking foolish or out of control?

Since all of my bottled-up emotions had to go somewhere, there was no amount of milk, cookies, or antacids that could prevent that ulcer from ravaging my insides. Early one morning when I was about 17, I woke before anyone else to use the bathroom. On my way back to my bedroom, I walked straight into a wall and collapsed, startling my parents out of bed. I was rushed to the hospital, where they discovered that my ulcer had perforated and I was bleeding internally. I had lost so much blood that I'd become anemic, and this is what had caused me to faint. I was given a blood transfusion and put on stronger medication to try to patch up the hole in my stomach. Luckily, I was able to return home and go back to school without missing too many classes.

With my ulcer under control for the time being, it was time to plan the next stage of my life. I was about to graduate from high school, and I knew that I wanted to go to university. Always the person who wanted to have total control, and being a great planner and organizer, I thought I'd developed a sound plan for my college career. In those days, our education system had only two streams: the academic and the technical. I was in the academic stream and had excelled in science and math, and wanted to continue proving myself in this arena. I was under the false impression that in order to continue hiding from my feelings, I had to further develop my mind. So it made sense that I should go to university and study the subjects that I was strongest in.

Part of my plan was to challenge myself, go to a very reputable university, and take the hardest courses available. This was consistent with my belief that the smarter I was, the more I would be recognized. After challenging my mind and honing it to brilliance, my plan was to return home and take over the family business. It all seemed quite logical, and even the guidance counselor I talked to agreed.

So off to the University of Toronto I went to get the most challenging post-secondary education available. I would excel, I was sure. After all, I'd earned excellent grades in high school and was ready to take on whatever this institution could throw my way. What a shock I was in for. After graduating with high A's in my high school math courses, I failed my first university math test. When I saw that F scrawled on top of my paper, I knew that something must have gone terribly wrong.

My first year in Toronto proved to be one of the most difficult experiences of my life. Coming from a small town and trying to survive in that huge urban center required some major adjustments. I truly was on my own as I tried to make friends and navigate the maze of my education. While I was fortunate to have some relatives who lived in the city, I still didn't feel I had the support I needed to help me cope. I remember seeking out the assistance of the university health clinic to talk to a psychiatrist. While it was supposed to help make things better, I typically left those sessions feeling worse, as if something were actually wrong with me. *Why am I not able to fit in anywhere I go? Why does everything in my life have to be so difficult?* I wondered.

I worked extremely hard, studied earnestly, and made a few friends. But mostly I felt lonely and isolated. It was difficult for me to partake in a typical social life because, besides the fact that I was somewhat shy and introverted, I was unable to consume any alcohol due to my ulcer. Drinking was a huge part of university culture, but I remained sober and put all my time and effort into studying. Although I didn't particularly like my classes, I remained committed to my goal of earning high grades. At the end of my first year, I'd managed to secure a 72 percent average—not close to the 90s I was used to getting in high school, but better than the failing grades I'd received at the start of the semester.

Despite the rise in my grades, partway through my first year I'd come to the realization that my whole university plan hadn't been very well thought out. I discovered that the University of Toronto had a wonderful and highly respected business and commerce program that I hadn't even considered. If I knew for sure that I was going into the family business, then why wasn't I enrolled there instead of in premed, which would be virtually useless to my chosen career path? Either the guidance counselor had forgotten to mention this option to me, or I'd been way too single-minded in my plans and missed it altogether. Either way, after enduring my first year of predominantly science and math classes, I decided that by jockeying around some courses for my second year I could switch into the commerce program. I returned to my hometown to work in the family business for the summer, somewhat relieved that I'd survived, albeit barely.

Before I knew it, the summer was over and it was time to return to Toronto and embark on this new program that I was hoping would be easier and more relevant. I really didn't want to leave work and go back to school, but I forced myself to continue with my studies.

Well, my wish had come true, and not only was my course load easier, it was also far more interesting. The economics, accounting, and business classes made so much more sense, and for the first time ever, school actually started to feel like fun.

So what was the problem? Being the driven, focused, and determined person that I was, I had begun to analyze my situation again: *How can I be here having fun, learning, and enjoying myself while my father is home working so hard in the family business?* Now that I was finally happy, I started to feel guilty. *I should be at home helping*, I told myself. I knew that I was going to end up there anyway, so why was I wasting my time in school? I decided that if I dropped out after my second year, I could get a head start on my practical learning back home. All of those ingrained beliefs began to rear their nasty heads, influencing my decision and preventing me from enjoying what was supposed to be a carefree experience.

But I had no time to waste having fun. I had things to accomplish, and I needed to get moving. My theory was that the sooner I began my career in business, the sooner I'd become very good at what I did, and the sooner my father would respect me as an equal. So at 21 years old, much to my mother's dismay, I dropped out of college and moved back in with my parents to begin what would become a 33-year career of building, expanding, and running our family business.

What my 21-year-old self wasn't aware of was that once you get in the habit of pushing for something new and exciting all the time, you can easily become dependent on the thrill of it. I was addicted to reaching the next big accomplishment. I always wanted more, expected more, and needed more in order to feel fulfilled. I was always in a huge hurry to reach and overcome the next hurdle. So there I was, working full time, driving hard to expand the business, and pushing for us to make more money, all the while trying to prove to myself and to everyone else that I was good enough.

I excelled in the world of business. Even though I'd never worked for anyone but my father and hadn't earned a university degree, I became a highly successful, self-taught entrepreneur. At the time, however, I was too busy trying to prove myself to acknowledge that I was good at what I did. Instead, my focus was always on what I wasn't doing well enough and what I needed to improve on in order to make things bigger and better. I was stuck in the all-too-common struggle of always striving but never arriving. My life had become an extension of what I believed, and so no matter how hard I worked, or how badly I wanted to achieve more, I would remain unsatisfied until I began to dig up those beliefs and really face them head-on.

The Belief Tree

Beliefs are like the roots of a tree. Some are thick and long and have been around for a long time, while others are skinny, short, and just beginning to establish themselves. From these roots grow a trunk, which is like our thoughts. The trunk grows branches, and these are like our words. These branches grow buds, which are like our actions. When these buds begin to bloom, they represent our life taking form. As we grow over time, it becomes clear that what we believe is the root of all that we create. Our successes, failures, joys, and sorrows all come about because of the beliefs that are holding us in place. Therefore, in order for any life experience to change, our root beliefs need to change first.

The business was expanding, and in working with my father I was finally getting lots of his attention. This was difficult for my mother, though, because since I was the only one of my siblings still living at home, most of our mealtimes and all of our spare time was spent discussing business. I knew she felt left out, but if that was what it took to get Dad's attention, then so be it. Now that we had something in common, he and I were able to form a very tight bond. We were partners in business. We never really had a father-son relationship, but I wasn't complaining. I'd settle for any connection that involved him noticing me.

My career was well on its way, and I knew I couldn't live at home for the rest of my life. The next step, according to the beliefs I'd adopted from my parents and society, was to find a wife, settle down, and start having kids. Marrying within my religion was important for me, and since there were virtually no Jewish women my age living in our town, I had to rely on meeting someone from another city. Because I wasn't overly friendly, I decided to let others set me up on blind dates. And so I set out on my search for the perfect partner. I actually had little idea as to what I was looking for in a wife, but I felt confident that I'd know her when I met her.

After what seemed like endless blind dates with all sorts of women, I finally met the one for me: a kindhearted, fun-loving teacher from Toronto. Though she lived about a five-hour drive away, I wasn't going to let distance stand in the way of achieving my next milestone. I met Lois in November, and by February we were engaged to be married. We both wanted the same things in life, and we were quite compatible on many levels. Although I thought that I was in love at the time (and I've come to know that I truly was), my understanding of love back then was certainly more mental than emotional. I know my wife must have truly loved me, because she left her family and career in Toronto to move to Pembroke, hundreds of miles away from the only life she had ever known.

Once we were married we moved in together, which was a bit of an adjustment for me, having never lived with anyone other than my parents. But other than the minor nuances of cohabitation, I was really very happy. That doesn't mean that I was no longer plagued by life's challenges—I was. It was just that for the first time, I finally had someone whom I loved and trusted and could share my frustrations, problems, and dilemmas with.

My wife was, and has remained for 32 years, my very best friend. She stood by me as I went through life's greatest challenges and greatest joys. I know that she put up with a lot, and at times I wasn't the easiest person to live with. How could I have been, given all that inner turmoil I still hadn't come to terms with? But we were able to work through our differences. It wasn't always peaceful or calm in our home, but we always came back to that love whenever things got too overwhelming. Now, all these decades later, we've both gone through our own spiritual awakening of sorts and are happier, more in love, and more respectful of one another than we ever were before. And, finally, I'm able to feel and express love from my heart rather than from my head, and this has made a world of a difference in our relationship.

Although my early life was in many ways quite typical, and my challenges not unlike those faced by many young people, what I believe makes my path unique is that I chose to change it. Until I was 50, I lived somewhat unconsciously—going through the motions, the ups and the downs, without stopping to reflect on or evaluate how I was feeling or why I felt a certain way. When I finally woke up and realized that something significant was missing in my life, everything changed. I had accomplished much, yet I felt a deep sense of discontentment, unhappiness, dissatisfaction, and restlessness. Although I didn't know it at the time, something within me was yearning for more. I began an intense journey of self-discovery that I'm still on today. I have learned much about myself, others, and the ways of the world. As a result, many of my behaviors have dramatically shifted, and I've overcome countless fears and self-limiting beliefs. My life has changed for the better, and now it's my greatest desire to awaken, empower, and inspire others. So I hope that in sharing my story, I have begun helping you find your own path to a better and more fulfilling life.

Chapter Two

FAMILY, FIREWORKS,
AND FRUSTRATIONS

Jeffrey's Story

January 2, 1981, was perhaps the second most important day of my life, the first being my wedding day. Lois and I had been married for less than two years, our life together was about to change forever, and I would learn more about myself and life than I ever could have imagined. It was a frigid winter in Pembroke, perhaps among the coldest in history. One of the first things I learned that day was that there's a point on both temperature scales (Fahrenheit and Celsius) where the temperature is the same—minus 40 degrees. It actually was that cold. But on the evening of January 2, a bundle of warmth and joy came into our lives. Our first child was born, a beautiful daughter. I was a father, and nothing would ever be the same again. I'm not sure why first-time parents aren't given the opportunity to learn more in advance, but I sure could have used some education. There are courses you can take and books you can read that help you understand how to physically care for babies, but what about some preparation for the emotional anxiety that besets new moms and dads when their first child comes into the world?

I've found that we all have behavioral characteristics that serve us well at times, but those very same traits can be a real detriment at other points. I tend to be quite optimistic and even naïve about my ability to handle whatever comes my way. That's not to say that there weren't times when fear brought about negative feelings, but I always assumed that no matter how many things I was attempting to juggle, I'd be fine.

Let me describe what was already going on in my life when our baby daughter came into the world. I'd been working in the family business since 1973, having begun to transition it from a scrap yard to a wholesale-distribution steel business. I had finally fulfilled my desire to settle down and get married. The next step was to start having kids. I have come to realize that much of what I thought I wanted in life didn't really come from my own conscious thought, but instead from what I had been taught by others.

Lois had always wanted to have kids; I knew that the moment we met. She was an excellent teacher, and her greatest love and passion in life was (and still is) children. She has been a fantastic mother, and without her, our sons and daughter would not have turned out as well as they did. I, too, wanted a family, but I'm certain that my passion for children wasn't the same. I came from a family of three kids, as did my wife. Having little ones was part of that long list of "should dos" that society and my parents expected of me—just like getting married, finding a good job, making lots of money, working hard, being smart, accumulating lots of possessions, proving my worth to others, staying well informed, giving back to the community, and providing a good life for my family . . . all in the name of happiness.

So, I was working extremely hard because I needed to prove that I was good enough, and I wanted the financial rewards that would allow me to provide for my growing family. I had to be the provider, and I had to be a good one. As I've mentioned, I'd developed a bit of a perfectionist attitude. Actually, I guess it was more than a bit—I was a big-time perfectionist. And so, this inner drive had me working 50 to 60 hours a week, becoming the president of a local service club, sitting on the board of the local chamber of commerce, and assuming the position of chairman of the city's planning board. *Of course I can do it all,* I thought. Not only was I the president of the Rotary Club, but I'd also earned perfect attendance for 17 years. Yes, anything worth doing was worth doing well. I was so driven that I was devastated when I didn't achieve a goal. Failure was not an option. I truly believed that I could do anything I set my mind to. If I pushed myself hard enough, I'd succeed.

This was where I was at when our first child entered the world. Unfortunately, along with our precious baby girl, 1981 also brought the beginning of the first economic recession that I'd have to face as the president of—up until then—a flourishing business. Life was about to get a whole lot more complicated, and I was completely unprepared.

I'm sure that some of you know what having a baby is all about, but I didn't have a clue as to what was in store. *I'm an intelligent and successful person, so what can be so difficult about taking care of a baby?* I thought. But in reality, she seemed so small and fragile, and carrying her was very different from lugging a piece of steel. I was afraid of holding this tiny, helpless little person. *What if I drop her? What if I squish her?* Thank heavens Lois was a natural mother. She made it look so easy, the way she held and nurtured our first child. I stood back and let her take the lead, not wanting to mess anything up, terrified of failing as a father.

Then there was the sleep deprivation. I don't function well without enough rest, so I had no idea how I'd manage our multi-million dollar business on just three to five hours of sleep a night. At this point, I began to realize that perhaps I wasn't actually as in control of it all as I thought I was. I wasn't acting like a very good partner to Lois, because I could not, or perhaps would not, do what she wanted me to. Maybe this was a result of my traditional belief system that said men were to be the providers and women the nurturers. Although these old-school beliefs had already begun to dissipate in society, I came from a family where they still held true. Maybe it was my lack of self-confidence in my ability to care for a baby, or it could have been that I truly had nothing left in me after working, volunteering, and stressing about all of my commitments. Nevertheless, I was not nearly as helpful or supportive as I could have been in those early parenting years.

It was a difficult time in my life and a challenging chapter in our marriage, but thank goodness we both subscribed to the belief that you always work on your marriage no matter how difficult the going gets, because the commitment lasts a lifetime. We were fortunate enough to have good role models in that area, as both sets of our parents had been together for years and withstood many challenges in their own relationships. We were determined to get through the sleepless nights, the pressures of business, the influence of family and friends telling us how to raise our children, and all of the other daily hurdles.

We adjusted to life with a baby, and after a few months decided that maybe it wasn't so bad after all. Sixteen months after our daughter, Hailey, was born, along came our first son, Allan. Now we had our "millionaire's family" (one boy and one girl), so all I had to do was earn a million dollars to provide for them. While parenting a new baby seemed a bit easier the second time around, the issue of my not doing enough to help out didn't disappear. Instead, we just tried to live with our differences of opinion. I assumed that the pressure and stress I was feeling were just a part of life and that there was no other way. I didn't know any better. *Life is supposed to be challenging if you want to get ahead,* I thought.

▩　▣　▨

With a second toddler running around, it became obvious that our home was too small for our growing family. It was time to move into a bigger and more family-friendly place. Although the economy was still struggling, we made the decision to build the house of our dreams. It seems I still hadn't learned that the more pressure I put upon myself, the worse I would feel about my life. So as with everything I did, I jumped into this new project headfirst, with the intention of not only overseeing the contractor I'd hired, but actually acting as the builder. There I was facing more work, more stress, and more pressure. The good news is that this time all my hard work paid off. The house was gorgeous, and everyone was pleased with the outcome. And once we had the home, it was time to fill it with another baby.

Although I thought I was coping fairly well with all the pressure and anxiety, apparently my body didn't think so. Shortly after moving, I was diagnosed with Crohn's disease. I had always experienced gastrointestinal issues, but I just thought it was part of my genetic makeup, so I was truly shocked when I received this diagnosis. After further testing to ensure that the medication for this disease would not cause greater harm to my ulcer, it was determined that I should go on steroids for a defined period of time to get the Crohn's under control. My wife and I decided that we'd better hurry up and conceive before I started taking the new drugs. I'm not sure I truly wanted a third child, primarily because I was starting to feel the physical effects of what I'd heaped upon myself for so many years. But Lois loved children, and she was a fantastic mother. I wanted to make her happy, so I convinced myself that one more wouldn't really make our lives all that different.

On June 16, 1985, our third baby was born. We named him Michael. He was very calm for the first year of his life, but then things changed. He came into this world with his own agenda. He wasn't going to be pushed around or made to do anything he didn't want to do. We didn't know this at the time, but Michael had a major issue with having his freedom taken away. He sure picked the wrong family if he wanted to run free! Or maybe he did pick the right family, because as it turned out, we were all about to learn many lessons that would eventually help us wake up to a more conscious life.

Our other two children were already growing up and learning how to behave by the time Michael came along. I can distinctly remember a time when Hailey and Allan were sitting quietly on the couch, probably having a time-out for getting too wound up. Along came Michael, not yet two, with a toy in hand ready to cause a ruckus. He started hitting both of his siblings on the head with the toy. He may have been the new kid in town, but he certainly wasn't going to let anyone forget that he was there! The dynamic of three children is quite different from that of two, and when one of the kids always wants things his way, life can become very challenging.

Although I'd declared to my wife that if we had a third child she shouldn't count on me for much help—I already felt that I had too much responsibility running the family business—when she became overwhelmed with Michael, she had no choice but to turn to me for support. Unfortunately, I just didn't have the energy or stamina to give her what she really needed. I was always trying to keep everyone happy and give of myself until there was nothing left, primarily because I had been raised to believe that it's better to give than to receive. It was as if I were walking around with a cup, tirelessly begging others to fill it with respect, validation, encouragement, and love, none of which I was able to give to myself. The harder I tried, the larger my cup seemed to grow, and the more impossible it became to fill it. I was always looking for the thank-you or the gold star that came from being a giving and caring person. But no matter how much praise I got, it never left me feeling fulfilled. That's because all of my generosity was actually coming from a place of obligation rather than love. And no external appreciation could fill the internal void that had been created by the lack of love I had for myself.

Related to this, living around the corner from, and working closely with, my father also had its challenges. Because I still had a deep desire to get recognition and love from him, I often felt torn between my family of origin and the nuclear family I'd created with Lois and the kids. He and I spent a lot of our free time talking business, and although I enjoyed this, I also wanted to be around for my wife and children. So when my dad would suggest that we go for a drive on a Sunday morning to talk, I felt torn. I often found myself choosing him over my family, in hopes of further gaining his approval. This did not go over well with my wife and kids. Trying to please everyone was not working out for me, or for them. It was an impossible mission that caused endless frustration and conflict.

❦ ❦ ❦

As our babies turned into little people, we had to start teaching them how to act, how to speak, and how to think—or so we thought. We didn't realize that we were simply passing on the same self-limiting beliefs that our parents had passed along to us. These ideas were the foundation of how we thought life should be lived. Although my wife and I didn't always subscribe to the same principles, we tried to remain as united as possible when teaching our kids the morals, values, and philosophies of life. Ironically, it's these same beliefs that I put so much effort into instilling in my children that years later I would try to help them undo.

At the time, I, like so many others, was afraid to do anything that was different from the norm. I was never empowered to search for and discover my own beliefs, because I lived within a family and society that encouraged conformity. While outwardly I may have had the freedom to think and act according to my own volition, internally I was afraid of going against the grain or standing out. And I passed on these same fears to my children, encouraging them to follow the same limiting beliefs that were governing my life.

For the next few years, Hailey, Allan, and Michael would come to learn that children must: *do as they are told, be well behaved, keep their rooms clean, do well in school (because without an education, they won't get anywhere in life), obey the rules (and if they don't, know there will be consequences), mind their manners, respect their elders, and realize that money doesn't grow on trees.* Sound familiar? Well, we didn't stop there. We also tried to instill that: *life isn't a walk in the park; you have to work hard to get ahead; you should always behave, because you don't want people to think poorly of you or your parents; those in authority know best; children should be seen and not heard; it's better to give than to receive; getting good grades in school is very important and will affect how you do in life; you shouldn't get too excited, because you'll just set yourself up for disappointment; you need to toughen up and compete to win; you shouldn't be too sensitive; and only the strong will survive.* Life sure sounds rough when you put it this way. But we honestly had no idea that we were filling our children with so many limitations and so much fear. We didn't know better.

All of this caused some resistance and conflict within our family; we were so focused on telling our kids what was in their best interest that we never thought to ask them how they were feeling. While many sons and daughters put up a bit of a fuss when their parents try to "train" them, Michael was a different story altogether. He had a mind of his own, and he was holding on to his freedom for dear life. He *was not* going to do what he was told, just because we said so. No, Michael had a resistance, a fight within him that was very different from our other children. He appeared to be my nemesis.

I had always been a fairly obedient child, and so far Hailey and Allan were growing up to be the same. So coming up against Michael's conviction was really unnerving. I believed that my children should simply do things *my way* or hit the highway. Thank goodness Lois was more understanding. In the early years, she was always there, defending Michael, although her patience was often tested also. She read every book on raising "difficult" and "spirited" children. At one point she even took him to a child psychiatrist in Ottawa to help us all cope with his refusal to follow the rules of society. It took a lot of effort to try to fit Michael's ways into our family dynamic.

I was still so busy with work that I didn't have time to be there for the kids. I would help them with their schoolwork, but I was not a very participatory father. Most evenings I came home from a challenging day at the office just in time for supper. I distinctly remember sitting at the table, my mind wandering off to review the events of a hectic day, while our children eagerly shared their stories and experiences. I pretended to listen, but I wasn't really present. I had bigger problems to worry about.

As Hailey, Allan, and Michael grew up and began to have minds of their own, I found myself in the midst of what often felt like an uprising or rebellion. It seemed harder and harder to keep the troops united. We couldn't even agree on a restaurant to go to on a Sunday evening. Although I didn't understand at the time, Michael was very sensitive to things around him, and as a boy he didn't handle change very well. I will never forget the time we went to a new restaurant and he ordered his typical chicken-finger dinner. When his meal came to the table, slightly less "fingery" and more "nuggety," he refused to even take a bite. These were not the chicken fingers he'd expected, and we therefore found ourselves in the midst of yet another temper tantrum and an embarrassing Sunday night out with the family. No one really knew how to cope with Michael or help him adapt to change.

When you have a challenging child, one thing you always get is lots of advice from family and friends. Everyone seemed to be an expert, and they all wanted to tell us how to deal with the situation. I was very used to the business world where I was in control, but a family that didn't go according to plan was something totally different and extremely hard to cope with.

Around this time, I also began to realize just how costly raising three children could be. There seemed to be an endless list of family expenses, including overnight camp, music lessons, sports teams, clothing, entertainment, vacations, and of course we had to have a pool in the backyard. The pressure to keep making lots of money was ever present.

"Work harder; we have so many expenses!" "Why aren't you around more helping with the kids and being a better father?" "All you do is work!" "Why are you spending time napping on the weekends instead of playing with your kids?" "I can't do this alone." I heard Lois saying all of this, but I was frustrated, overwhelmed, pressured, stressed, exhausted, and emotionally drained. I'm not saying that the challenges I faced as a father were any worse than what others go through, nor am I trying to elicit sympathy here. It's just that in the moment, when things seemed so out of my control, I didn't really stop to think, or care, about the big picture. I just needed a nap—a very long nap.

Michael's Story

I believe that I was born with a very powerful purpose. It took me until I was about a year old to discover what that was: causing trouble, questioning everything, and not listening to anyone except myself. My mom actually referred to my first year of life as "the calm before the storm." Back then, she says, I was quiet and peaceful, observing the world around me. Once I figured out how to walk, however, there was no stopping me from fulfilling my purpose. That was when all the fun began! Once the "terrible twos" arrived early, they stuck around until I was about 13. It became a joke that my family told at my bar mitzvah, and although it was delivered in a loving way, it was confirmation that my early years were by no means an easy ride.

Back then I certainly marched to the beat of my own drum. I never understood why life had so many rules and why they needed to be followed so strictly, especially since they made me so unhappy. I felt as though I was always being labeled, and this continued into my teenage years. I was given my first label as a young child, and it stuck with me for a long time. I was called the "spirited child," which was really a polite way of saying, "This kid doesn't listen to anyone, and he lives in his own world with his own set of guidelines." I appreciate my mom for coming up with this relatively polite title; however, I heard many other, less-kind variations of it when I did something that upset her.

Being identified as "spirited," "challenging," or "difficult" caused me to question my identity. I was always being labeled according to what others saw in me, but never given the chance to really discover who I actually was or wanted to be. At the time, I felt mostly judgment, ridicule, and shame coming from family members, peers, and society. Everyone, it seemed, wanted to change me and turn me into a "normal" kid. At that young age, I had a choice to either fight back or internalize it all and accept it as true. Since I wasn't someone who just stood by and watched, I chose to fight. And I did a pretty good job of it, too.

Back then it felt as if it were me against the world. If I gave in to the demands of others, then I'd be allowing them to turn me into somebody I didn't want to be. So every time my parents asked me to do something, my immediate answer was, "No!" I knew from the time I was small that I wasn't here to be a pushover, and once that flame was lit inside me, I had no idea what to do with it other than to rebel.

I remember that one of my favorite games used to be banging on my siblings' bedroom doors as loudly as I could and then hiding. They knew who it was, but could never find me once they got up and opened their doors. Then when I finally got bored, I would let them catch me. This was typically followed by both my brother and sister screaming in unison, as if they had rehearsed it: "Mom, Michael is bothering us again!" I would smile, waiting for the validation that I had completed my job. As if on cue, my mom would respond, "Michael, go to your room." This phrase was something I came to hear over and over throughout my childhood.

Even when I wasn't actually doing anything wrong, my family still blamed me for everything. To this day, these tendencies still subtly come out when we all get together. I became the scapegoat at a young age, and the more everyone dwelled on my bad behavior, the more I rebelled against them by acting out even more. The focus seemed to always be on all of the things I did wrong, and all the ways I wasn't "normal," so as a result I refused to change.

Getting me to go to my room and stay there was not an easy task. My parents had to install a lock on the outside of my bedroom door to keep me in there at times. I'd heard of kids wanting a lock on the inside of the door to give them more privacy, but I'm pretty sure I was the only one who had a lock on the outside to prevent me from getting out. I remember my parents always used to say, "Go to your room and think about what you've done. You can't come out until you've learned your lesson." In hindsight, what they were saying makes sense, but at that age I was never taught how to learn from my behavior, or how to reflect on those lessons so I could grow as an individual. If I'd been given some practical tools and strategies at a young age, I might have listened, learned, and possibly even changed as a result.

To be completely honest, at the time I didn't even realize that change was within my power. I had given up all personal responsibility, heaping the blame on my parents, teachers, siblings, and anyone else who got in my way and tried to tell me what to do. I always felt as if life was happening *to* me, but I've come to realize now that life happens *for* me. The principle of personal responsibility states that we have a hand in creating everything in our lives. Those who believe in this wholeheartedly take it to mean that no matter what happens—good or bad—they play a role in attracting it. It can be incredibly empowering to know that we have the ability to create positive and rewarding experiences. My childhood probably would have been much less traumatic if I'd had the opportunity to learn this lesson sooner, but I was still trapped in the cycle of blame and excuses.

My parents constantly assumed that I would learn my lesson, so I often played along with their game and told them what they wanted to hear. "I promise I won't do it again," was a common response I'd use to get myself out of sticky situations. I knew that if I looked serious enough or sad enough, my mom would eventually cave and let me out. However, as the years passed and I kept saying the same things without showing any real change in my behavior, they started to catch on, and it took a lot more effort to convince them I was being sincere. In fact, the communication on both ends was full of threats and promises, without a whole lot of follow through by any of us.

Are You *Responsible* for Your Life?

A prerequisite for living a conscious life is taking personal responsibility for your thoughts, words, actions, habits, choices, and relationships. Although some things may be out of your control, what you do possess, no matter what, is the ability to choose how you respond to anything that comes your way. *Taking responsibility means accepting that you have the power to create the life you truly want.* If you pass off this responsibility, deny your power, or blame others for the choices you make, you'll find it increasingly difficult to live a happy life.

My dad wasn't around much when I was young. He was too busy running the family business and didn't have the time or energy to really be there for me as a father. The only thing he did do very well was say *no*. I remember very distinctly that if I asked my dad for anything, 99 percent of the time his first answer was always, "No." Sometimes I'd get a "Go ask your mother," and that's when I knew I'd have a better chance of getting what I wanted. I learned very quickly that if I wanted something, I'd have to get my mom's approval, and then she'd convince my father to give in. While I alone couldn't convince Dad of anything, Mom had special powers for that.

At the time, my mom became my only source of love, affection, and support. But she was also the master of pushing my buttons and throwing out idle threats in response to my behavior. I lost track of how many times I heard, "Michael, if you don't smarten up, we're going to send you away to boarding school," or "Michael, if you don't learn how to behave, I'm going to drive you down to the Columbus House immediately." (The Columbus House was a facility for troubled youth who couldn't get along with their parents.)

I was a very astute kid, and I learned from what I observed around me. I saw that my mom loved me so much that she wanted to turn me into a "normal" child who followed orders and fit into society and our family. She also felt that if I didn't learn discipline at a young age, I would never follow any rules as I got older, and could potentially wind up as a menace to society or even a criminal. It was her biggest fear that I would end up in jail or be viewed as a delinquent in the eyes of others. She was never afraid to express her feelings to me. I heard it all: the threats, the promises, the angry comments, and all the arguing about me that my parents did late at night, their voices carrying through the thin walls of our adjoining rooms. In fact, sometimes my siblings even told me that Mom and Dad's arguing was my fault. That one was a tough pill to swallow. I never wanted to actually cause harm to anyone around me; I was only doing what I thought would make me feel better at the time. Although my mother and I butted heads more often than not, she was still able to balance our conflict with tons of love and affection, and I can only imagine what my childhood would have been like if not for that.

Another challenge I faced growing up was that it seemed as if everyone was trying to make decisions for me, which were based on their own values and beliefs and very rarely had my own best interests in mind. I hated this because I thought that life was supposed to be fun, and I was determined to live in whatever way made me happy. This was often the cause of struggle at home. My dad always needed to believe that he had control over everything, so as a result he would do his very best to lay down the law on a regular basis. One of his famous sayings was, "As long as you live in my household, you have to follow my rules. If you don't like it, live somewhere else." He knew very well I was way too young to actually pick up and move out. As independent as I thought I was, I was still very much dependent on my parents for the basic needs of survival. This is how all my anger started to form, because every time he made a comment like that, I felt as though my freedom were being completely stripped away from me. I didn't even have a say in the matter. *Why does he get to make all the decisions for me?* I fumed. *He doesn't even know me!*

I remember thinking that a lot of things were unfair and that I was getting the short end of the stick. I was told that I was too young to know what was best for me, and that because my parents were older and had experienced more, they knew better. I was never empowered to make my own decisions, and I was rarely asked how I felt about a situation. Being the fighter that I was, I wouldn't stand for it. I wasn't going to be someone who got pushed aside and told what to do. So I rebelled with all of my might. Verbally, physically, emotionally—in any way I could—I fought back against my parents, against the system, and against anyone who told me what to do. What nobody realized at the time was that all this could have been avoided if they'd simply taken the time to not only ask me what I thought, but to empower me to be a part of the process of my own life. Even though it may have seemed like it, I wasn't actually demanding complete freedom to do whatever I pleased. I was simply looking for guidance and support so that I could begin to start making decisions for myself.

Take my messy bedroom, for example. This drove my parents crazy, especially my father, who was a control freak *and* a neat freak. In fact, it wasn't just my room that I left a mess. I never hung up my jacket, I never washed the dishes after I used them, and I never took the time to clean up after myself in general. However, I probably would have been more inclined to do so if I were empowered to make that choice for myself.

Part of my reason for being messy was a form of rebellion against what I was being told to do: "Michael, clean your room," "Michael, pick up your jacket," "Michael, put the food back in the fridge when you're done with it." I heard it all, and the more they said it, the angrier I got. I was always being told what I had to do, but was never given the power to decide for myself. It was simply a matter of semantics.

Instead of telling me what to do all the time, perhaps they could have found a better approach that didn't trigger so much aggression. Maybe they could have communicated in a way that expressed their desires rather than their demands. Maybe they could have attempted to understand why I wasn't cleaning up after myself and tried to help me see from their perspective why cleanliness was actually important. And then, if necessary, maybe they could have provided gentle boundaries for consequences if I didn't show respect for their wishes. Perhaps then things would have been different.

Instead, my mom and dad made their demands, and I retaliated by asking, "Why?" Their response was typically: "Because I said so," or "Because we're the parents, and those are our rules." From their perspective, kids weren't supposed to question what their parents said; they were just supposed to go with it. The ironic part is that I didn't even like things messy. In fact, I preferred them organized, but by my own standards, not my parents'. If we'd only been able to communicate this to each other at the time, life could have been much less complicated. But we chose the hard way, and nothing was simple in my house as a result. In fact, nothing was simple in my childhood.

It's All about Perspective!

Have you ever felt like no one understands you? That no matter how much you try to explain what you mean, no one seems to get it? You feel frustrated and think, *If I understand, why can't they?* This is what I went through during the first 18 years of my life. I saw things in a way no one else could and had trouble getting others to view them from my perspective. While I felt completely alone and misunderstood, I only realized later that most people experience the same thing at some point. Most of us have a deep desire to be understood, and while we often expect others to fully comprehend what we're saying and see things our way, this is actually impossible. We all possess a unique perspective that cannot be shared or replicated. No two people see the world in the exact same way. This can be quite frustrating, especially when we're trying to communicate how we feel, what we see, or what we're experiencing. If we're able to understand perspective, however, we can find ways to get around this frustration.

When I talk about *perspective*, I'm referring to the vantage point from which you see life. It is the lens or filter that you look through. Each perspective is made up of individual experiences and emotions. It doesn't remain stagnate; just as experiences and beliefs change, so too does perspective. This shift can happen throughout a lifetime or in the course of a day. Your altering moods or emotions can influence you as much as your beliefs or values can.

One of the reasons I butted heads with other people was because I believed they should see the world as I did. Instead of trying to understand things from their points of view, I assumed that with enough persuasion they'd finally come to see things as I did. My obsession with being right often prevented me from shifting my perspective to incorporate their thoughts and opinions. As a result, I was constantly getting into power struggles, unwilling to waver in my views.

For me, the freedom I was longing for would only come when I was able to admit that everyone sees life through a different set of lenses, and no one perspective is ever right or wrong.

As I've already mentioned, the more everyone told me what to do, the angrier I got, because I understood this as them taking away what I needed most: my freedom. I also realized that in order to get what I truly desired, I'd have to look out for my own best interests. No one could stop me when I had my mind set on something. No one could prevent me from doing what I wanted. My guard was up, and I was ready to protect myself at whatever cost. The result was manipulative behavior that continued into my teenage years, and which eventually pushed my family farther away as I tried desperately to hold on to my independence.

I was, and still am, extremely sensitive, both emotionally and physically. This not only got in the way of my relationships with my family members and friends, but also made everything in my life seem more dramatic and difficult. It was never really explained to me what emotions were all about, nor was I taught how to express them in a responsible way. I thought that because I was a boy, I wasn't supposed to express myself, or I'd be seen as weak. Therefore, I did my best to control my sensitivity and never let it get out of hand.

So being the one who naturally rebelled against everything, I developed my own way of expressing my emotions. I was *that* kid who, in the middle of a shopping mall, restaurant, busy street, or amusement park, would throw a massive temper tantrum that would rock the sound waves and attract unwanted attention. I experienced uncontrollable anger that came over me from a variety of different triggers I was unaware of at the time. As I got a little older, I tried to control it and keep it under wraps, but that never really worked. As a result, when the anger did bubble to the surface, it was stronger and more explosive.

My mom and dad were so embarrassed by the scenes I caused that they spent a lot of time feeling on edge when we were in public. They feared that my tantrums were a reflection of their parenting abilities. I remember that my mom always begged me to be quiet so that others wouldn't hear me. But this just caused me to be louder and more dramatic, because no one was going to tell me what do.

A Trunk Full of Emotions

We're taught to only engage in "good" emotions, but what happens to the "bad" ones? Since we don't want to feel them, we often stop their natural flow, forcing them to get stuck in our bodies. Let's take anger, for example—we're taught that this is a bad emotion. Instead of feeling and expressing it when it first comes up, we often resist it. *It's like we put our anger in a trunk and lock it away—deep within us.* Every time another negative emotion comes up, it goes into the same place. But even within this trunk, the feelings are moving and stirring about. Picture it getting fuller by the day, each emotion pushing against the next, bouncing off the walls, eager to get out. Finally, the trunk can't resist the energy, and it explodes. What happens next depends on how you react. If you choose to keep resisting these emotions and force them back into the trunk, they may begin to turn into sickness or dis-ease within your body (more on this later). If you're unable to resist the emotions, you'll likely express them in unhealthy and irresponsible ways that often end up hurting you and others around you. This is where physical violence and verbal abuse come from.

When it came to being physically sensitive, my biggest challenge was with clothes. I couldn't wear any shirt with a printed logo or design that I could feel against my skin. My mom was extremely understanding and supportive of this sensitivity, and the summer before fifth grade, she took me shopping in Ottawa. We found one store with shirts that actually felt comfortable to me, so I bought five and wore those in rotation all year long. I faced a lot of ridicule from my peers that year when they caught on that I was wearing the same shirts over and over again. There was another occasion when I was getting ready to play street hockey with my friends, and it took me so long to get into my rollerblades and uncomfortable equipment that the game was over by the time I was ready. I was heartbroken.

I lost count of how many times my heart was broken growing up. Whether it was from emotional wounds, embarrassing experiences, or verbal attacks from my peers, it all felt so terrible and was really hard to recover from. Unfortunately, I didn't know how to deal with my sensitivity and had no one in my life whom I could look to for advice, so I eventually developed deep-rooted anger and frustration from these situations. I was known for having a short fuse, both on the playground and in my home. I'd spent so many years judging, suppressing, and not understanding all I was feeling, that when the anger built up in my trunk, it needed to be let out.

For the most part, I expressed it verbally, because I was so afraid of physical confrontation due to my heightened sensitivity to pain or discomfort. I remember dreaming of beating up all the people who were bothering me, but I never was able to do it when I was awake. Instead, I used words that were foul and abusive, and once I started on a tirade, I didn't know how to stop. This got me in trouble at school and created quite a rift with my parents. I was never taught how to cope with my anger or express it in an empowering way. Looking back, I think that if I'd had the opportunity to understand my emotions and learned to express myself more freely and responsibly from a young age, the explosions would not have been so intense. (See the Resources section at the end of this book for tips on how to express emotion in a healthy way.)

🈁 🔲 🈁

Unlike many kids my age, I also had no idea how to cope with change. In fact, I hated it and would have liked everything in my life to be predictable and consistent. If something did not appear as I saw it in my mind, then the fireworks went off instantly. This happened quite frequently at restaurants. As my Dad mentioned, I tended to order the exact same meal every time we went out to eat. My mom caught on to this fear and began preparing me as best she could for any new or unpredictable situation. I soon developed habits that allowed me to feel more safe and secure, but I was unaware that I was actually just covering up this problem with a Band-Aid. That fear of change stayed with me for my entire childhood, and it often showed up at inopportune times.

I played a lot of sports and was actually quite a good athlete, so this was one area where I actually felt like I belonged. However, my issues with change impacted my ability to have fun. One day I was at a local park playing baseball, and everything was going smoothly until a couple of new players showed up and asked to join the game. Everyone agreed except for me, because I didn't want the experience to change. The disruption was too much for me to handle, and I ended up running inside, crying to my parents, and refusing to go back out because the game (as I saw it) was completely ruined.

My mom always felt heartbroken when she saw me react this way; she had such deep empathy for what I put myself through and felt helpless because no matter how hard she tried, there was nothing she could do to fix the situation. I was easily devastated by things that seemed so easy for others to adapt to, and my life was being ruled by this inability to go with the flow.

And so I'd spend a lot of time alone in my room, where I felt safe. I'd talk out loud to myself, trying to process my feelings. Most of the time, I was both extremely angry and frustrated for having lost my freedom and being misunderstood. I felt scared, alone, and isolated.

The Fear Factor

Have you ever stopped to think about the impact fear has on *your* life? What are you most afraid of? Does it prevent you from succeeding in life or stop you from experiencing new things? Does it limit the people you meet or the conversations you have?

Fear is one of the most debilitating emotions—I learned this at a very young age. It robs us of our power and often leaves us feeling helpless. The emotion can come up whether the threat we're experiencing is real or imagined. For me, the story I created in my head about what any change might do to my existence was the most crippling. While none of the threats were actually real, they sure did seem that way at the time.

In our small town, my choice of friends was limited, and so I often found myself hanging out with people who were completely unlike me. Although I tried desperately to blend in with them, something always happened to remind me that I was an outsider. At the time, I based my self-worth and value on what others thought of me and their willingness to accept and validate me. If they didn't see me as "normal" and allow me to be a part of the "cool group," then I felt ashamed and worthless.

When I reached sixth grade, I finally was part of the popular group at school. It felt so wonderful to belong and know that I finally had friends who seemed to like me. I was able to use my athletic skills to gain acceptance and validation from my peers. I was also in the French-immersion stream, and so I was considered, by default, to be one of the smart kids. I attached my whole identity to the labels *athletic* and *intelligent,* and that stayed with me for a very long time. For a couple of years, life at school was, all things considered, quite pleasant. I was invited to parties and other social gatherings, I did well in sports, and I got good grades. Then, at the start of eighth grade, everything came crashing down.

Living in a relatively homogenous community presented a challenge for me that didn't surface until around this time. We were one of just a few Jewish families in a town that was predominantly Christian. In the Jewish faith when a boy turns 13, he has a bar mitzvah, and it was right before I started eighth grade that I had mine.

We had a huge party to celebrate this rite of passage, but I wasn't able to include all the students in my class. Once school started again, the kids who weren't invited decided to get all of my friends to turn against me, using the fact that I was Jewish as their ammunition. That whole school year became a devastating blow to my self-esteem and self-confidence. I lost all the validation and acceptance that I'd worked so hard to receive from my peers in previous years. I had to deal with rude, anti-Semitic remarks coupled with the pain of feeling isolated and alone.

I remember getting my mom to drive me to school at the last possible minute so I'd arrive just when the bell rang and avoid being seen alone in the school yard. During recess, I'd hide in the bathroom whenever possible in order to dodge the ridicule that I felt when I was outside. When I got up the courage to approach my old friends, they'd hit me with a barrage of verbal abuse or pretend I didn't exist. All of this made me so self-conscious that I ended up feeling afraid to express myself at all. I rarely spoke up in class and kept to myself as much as possible.

The only place I felt safe was at home, and my mom was the only person I could talk to. Even with her, I wasn't able to share half of what was going on inside of me. I remember talking to myself, because it was the only way I could articulate my feelings and maintain my sanity. I simply needed an outlet to express my emotions without judgment.

Finally, in the last few months of the school year, I started spending time with two kids who lived on my street, and even began to hang around with them at school. Even though my loneliness began to dissipate, I never really got over the emotional trauma. I ended up burying these wounds deep beneath the surface and went into high school hoping to get a fresh start and leave all the drama behind.

Chapter Three

SEARCHING FOR MEANING
IN THE TEENAGE STORM

Michael's Story

In bringing the Youth Wellness Network's wellness programs to high schools, I've come to realize that certain things are constant, no matter where you live or what decade you live in. One such thing is that high school is often a difficult, unsettling time for most young people. No matter if you're part of the in crowd or struggling to establish your place in a social circle, adolescence is wrought with challenges. In sharing my high-school experiences, I hope to make other young people realize that no matter what they're going through, or have gone through, they're not alone. The most important thing educators and parents can do for students is help them to realize that the more they're able to love themselves during this time, the better off they'll be. If I had cared more for myself as a teen, I'm positive that most of my troubles would have been much easier to deal with. But life is a wonderful journey, and because of what I experienced, I'm now driven to share my most valuable lessons with youth across the world in hopes that they don't have to endure what I did.

When I started high school, most of the challenges I'd been facing at home in my younger years were pushed aside to make room for the teenage drama that came to occupy my thoughts. I struggled to make and keep friends, while desperately trying to figure out who I truly was and who I wanted to be. I disconnected from my parents and family quite a bit, and although there were still some issues at home, they felt significantly less important compared to what was going on at school.

The chance to start over in high school was both extremely scary and exciting. I was hoping to leave behind a lot of the drama that happened in my last year of grade school and begin fresh with new people, a new environment, and a fresh outlook on life. This was also extremely nerve-wracking, because my confidence was already shaky, and I had no idea what to expect. I did, however, have one friend by my side throughout this new experience, so I clung to him as hard as I could in order to feel more secure throughout the process. His name was Steven, and he lived across the street from me. We'd always played sports together after school, but by the end of eighth grade, we'd begun hanging out at school as well. I felt more confident going to high school knowing that I at least had one person to tackle this new phase of life with.

I remember the first day as if it were yesterday, that I could hardly eat breakfast that morning because I was so nervous. I felt completely vulnerable. When it came time to get our locker assignments, I realized that mine and Steven's were at opposite ends of the building, so I decided to forgo the one I'd been assigned and chose the locker right beside his instead. Luckily, no one seemed to notice or care, and I made it through my first day without any major problems. But all of that would change, and I was totally unprepared for what lay ahead.

Ninth grade was a very interesting year for me, because on some level all I wanted to do was break out of my shell and start to figure out who I really was. At the same time, I was scared to do anything that would make me stand out or appear different, so the fear of being judged and ridiculed was still very much a factor behind all my actions and decisions. For the first few months of school, I relied on Steven like a life preserver, desperate not to feel the loneliness I'd experienced the previous year.

I wanted to branch out and meet some new people but was afraid to do it alone, so I convinced my friend to come with me as I ventured to find a group to fit in with. We came across a group of kids who were from even smaller towns than Pembroke. They had gone to a different grade school, so it was a fresh start for all of us. We became fairly close with some of the guys, and I was starting to feel a sense of belonging again. The challenge was that since I'd developed a real fear of expressing myself and was so afraid of standing out, I never developed my own opinions or expressed my true feelings. As a result, the relationships I had with my new friends were totally inauthentic. I tried my best just to float under the radar and fit in with the group, simply going along with whatever they said and did. For the most part, I tolerated this because it was way better than feeling that awful embarrassment of being alone. However, I knew I wasn't being true to myself, because I spent a lot of time feeling sad, uncomfortable, and stifled. But what would I have felt like if I were actually being authentic?

The Authentic Self

To be your authentic self is to be in a place of alignment where everything you say and do feels right. It's as if you're in the flow of a river, moving gracefully downstream, maneuvering easily around any obstacle that gets in your way. It's like sitting in front of a fire on a cold winter day, curled up reading your favorite book. It's like being in the presence of people who really like you and truly understand you. When you're in your authentic self, you feel comfortable, secure, loved, understood, and at ease.

> I have come to realize that the search to be truly authentic is a never-ending journey. The more we come to understand ourselves, the more we discover who we are, what we truly feel, and what makes us tick. And all of this changes with time and experience.

There was one place where I felt truly alive and authentic during my first year of high school, and that was on the basketball court. I'd fallen in love with sports as a child and played as often as I could. I always longed for the opportunity to be on a team, but because of where I lived, the only chance I had prior to high school was to join a summer soccer league.

My true passion was basketball, however, and finally in ninth grade I was able to play on a real team. Since I was a good athlete, playing ball allowed me to regain some of the self-worth and self-confidence that was lacking in other areas of my life. Something was different when I stepped onto the court; it was as if all my troubles melted away and the only thing that mattered was the game. For a while, I was convinced that this sport was my life, and I dreamed of becoming a professional. I worked extra hard in practice and spent every moment I could on the court.

I was longing for any validation or respect I could get. Now that I was part of the team, I finally felt accepted—but I wanted more. I wanted to be recognized, praised, and congratulated, all things I'd never learned how to give myself. The natural place to look for this was my teammates and coaches. My goal was to be recognized as the star player in every game and for every team I played on. If I didn't score the most points or wasn't named the most valuable player (MVP), I was a failure. As a result, I became extremely competitive, and a lot of the fun of playing sports began to slip away. This attitude stayed with me throughout each year of high school and on each new team I played for. Well, I never ended up winning the MVP award, and I never really got the validation and respect I was starving for. I held a grudge against my coaches and sometimes even my teammates for not giving me the recognition I felt I deserved. I always thought I was getting the short end of the stick, and once again found myself feeling isolated and alone—like no one understood me.

But truth be told, even if they'd praised me on the court, I likely wouldn't have noticed anyway. I was so down on myself and so untrue to who I really was that I wasn't open to love in any form. I didn't care for myself at the time, so therefore no external support could improve my situation. I was fighting a losing battle.

As ninth grade neared its end, I was feeling lost, unappreciated, and unrecognized. I longed for more than just fitting in. I wanted to be great, and I wanted everyone to respect me for my greatness. Instead of looking inward and learning to love myself (which I truly didn't realize was an option), I looked outward and wished that others would help build up my self-esteem, self-confidence, and self-worth.

▦ ▣ ▦

As I entered my second year of high school, I started to feel a bit more comfortable. No longer a member of the youngest grade in the school, I felt like I had a bit more authority. I was ready to start developing my image.

My physical appearance had been a challenge since I was a little kid. When I was young, I went through a chubby phase and became quite self-conscious about how I looked. This carried forward all those years and became even more important when I was in high school. In order to be someone cool who was worth getting to know, I felt I had to look good. As a result, I became obsessed with my appearance and spent way too much time in front of the mirror in the mornings, styling my hair with gel and getting totally frustrated when every curl didn't go in the direction I wanted it to. I was always striving to look better, cooler, and more special so I could get the respect and validation I believed I deserved.

This obsession was a big part of what made tenth grade so difficult for me. It was also my first experience with a four-letter word that almost every teenager dreads: acne! Many adolescents have breakouts at some point, but for some reason my case was much worse. At least that's how it felt at the time. There was a point when it got so bad that I didn't even want to look at myself in the mirror anymore. I'd load my face up with cover-up every day just so I could face my reflection. It was a horrifying blow to my self-esteem. My biggest fear was that my friends would think that I wore makeup to make the blemishes look better. It absolutely wasn't something guys were supposed to do. When I was finally discovered, it was devastating, and I felt so embarrassed and ashamed.

Finally, I went to my mom, desperate for help. She suggested I see a doctor to hopefully find a solution. My dermatologist recommended an anti-acne drug called Accutane. This was by far the most powerful product on the market; however, there happened to be a long list of possible side effects, and some were pretty serious. I decided to take the risk and signed up for the three-month dose that was required for the drug to start working. I was committed to getting this problem to go away, as I'd convinced myself that my confidence would return when my face was clear. I could *never* feel good about myself with a face full of zits!

Luckily, I didn't experience the predicted side effects, except for some extremely dry skin. For the next three months I obsessed over my complexion, spending every second I could examining my reflection, hoping and praying that I was getting better. After this time of my face being as dry as a desert, the acne not only got better, but for the most part disappeared completely. It was a miracle! From that point on, aside from the occasional blemish here and there, my face was clear. Although there were some scars, I was assured that they'd fade over time. I finally looked like myself again.

But sadly, my gratitude didn't last very long. Instead, I unconsciously started to judge other parts of my body. Nothing about me was ever good enough. No matter how I may have appeared, I was always criticizing myself about something, and, as a result, I attracted more judgment from everyone else. I didn't realize at the time that however I treated myself would always be reflected back to me, often with more intensity, by friends and peers. The more I judged myself, the more I was judged by others.

Around this time, I was really beginning to grow tired of not fitting in for who I truly was. But this was a catch-22—if I continued to fly under the radar, I'd face less judgment from others; but trying to go unnoticed and suppressing my true opinions and emotions made me feel much worse about myself. The more I allowed the fear of ridicule to take over, the more uncomfortable I was truly expressing how I felt and what I thought. Before I ever opened my mouth, I'd ask myself: *Are you sure you want to say that?* Typically the answer was, *No,* so I'd opt to remain silent, suppressing myself in order to remain neutral.

Sadly, this meant I even stifled some of my natural talents—including my singing ability. I have a great voice, a gift that wasn't bestowed on any other member of my family, but I never sang outside of my bedroom. I was so afraid of what others would think that I pretended I didn't have a good voice and got angry any time someone in my family asked me to sing.

Today I love to sing. I sing in the shower, to my niece and nephew, and while I'm walking down the street. Back in high school, I had no idea what my authentic self looked like, and so most of the time I pretended to be another person—someone who was cool and part of the in crowd. I even shaped my behaviors based on how others acted, hoping no one would suspect that I was different. Only later on did I finally uncover my true self, a person who speaks with conviction, isn't afraid to share his ideas and thoughts, and cares much less about what others think.

Uncovering Your Authentic Self

Since each human being is unique, one person's authentic self will always be different from another's. It's important to feel confident in your uniqueness. Unless you're prepared to let go of the pressure to fit in, it will be hard to identify who you truly are. Begin by getting familiar with your characteristics. It's critical, at this point, to drop all judgments. Things are no longer good or bad—they just are.

Most of us have been taught that our strengths are good and our weaknesses are bad. We've been taught that we should improve on our weaknesses or fix them. But what if those personality traits that others identify as problems actually feel okay to us? For example, being *disorganized* can also be seen as *flexible* and *free*. Being *flaky* or *ditsy* can also be seen as *happy* and *giddy*. Being *rigid* can also be seen as *focused* and *driven*. If we give up these attributes because others judge them as negative, does this not mean that we're denying our true self? The things we feel comfortable with are what make up our authentic self, not the ones others tell us we *should* feel good about.

In order to find your authentic self, it's important to better understand your own characteristics and behaviors. There is an ancient document of Hermetic teachings called *The Kybalion,* and one of the seven principles in this document is titled the Principle of Polarity. It embodies the idea that "everything is dual; everything has poles; everything has its pair of opposites." When you look at two things that appear to be opposites, *The Kybalion* tells us that what you're really seeing are two extremes of the same thing existing in a continuum. Take *hot* and *cold*—both are extreme forms of temperature with varying degrees in between (cool and warm, for example). Because there is no finite definition of *hot* or *cold*, it's difficult for people to agree on what each should feel like. What each person experiences, then, is based on his or her perception.

This is the same for human character traits. Some have a greater tendency to be responsible, while others are more irresponsible. Once you've given up on judging either of these as good or bad, you can try to get a sense of where you fit on the continuum. If you tend to lean more toward irresponsibility, then ask yourself: *How do I feel about this aspect of myself?* If you're comfortable with this quality, then it may very well be part of your authentic self. Keep in mind that all traits have positive and negative aspects. Being too responsible can have its drawbacks, just as being too irresponsible can. The object here is to become familiar with all of your characteristics and check in to determine how you feel about them.

On the other hand, there may be some traits you know that you possess but don't feel good about. For example, you may find yourself embarrassed and self-conscious around others, as I did throughout high school. You're likely unsure of where these apprehensions come from, but you know they don't seem natural to you. When you're in a place of embarrassment, you typically don't feel good, which means that you are out of alignment with your true, genuine self. While you don't need to be self-conscious when speaking up in a group, and there is no reason to feel embarrassed any time you're singled out, your subconscious brings up this response automatically. Until you're able to shift toward a place of self-love and confidence, you'll continue to come off as an insecure and awkward person—even though that's not who you truly are.

Once you're able to identify these characteristics, you may choose to dig deeper and search for the underlying issue that has caused this part of you to become out of alignment. Maybe you were once singled out in a crowd and made to feel foolish and insignificant. Or perhaps once when you did take a chance and speak your mind, you were shut down and criticized. Until you can make peace with your past and forgive those who hurt you, you'll continue to be haunted by these experiences and have trouble expressing yourself or taking a stand. But once you do the inner work to overcome whatever it was that brought about this inauthentic character trait, you'll be free to live more authentically as the confident, free, and happy person you truly are.

As tenth grade progressed, I became more and more fed up with myself for staying quiet and unnoticed. The embarrassment and self-consciousness that came up automatically were really starting to get on my nerves. I felt as if I were a leader and that I was destined for something greater than what I was experiencing, but I was too afraid to do anything about it. Finally, I got so tired of keeping my mouth shut that I started to release my suppressed emotions and opinions. And the results weren't pretty.

Since I'd stifled my own voice for so long, when I finally decided to express myself, all that came out was anger. I started bad-mouthing people behind their backs, because I was afraid to say how I felt to their faces. The only way I thought I could express myself was through words, and just as I'd developed a potty mouth as a child, I found myself speaking rudely and with haste. I shouted out in class. I cracked mean jokes and made fun of other people. I talked back to my parents. I wasn't a nice person to be around.

And the more I tried to defend myself with words, the more I was attacked with even harsher ones. This was the beginning of some very challenging times for me. I happened to be the only Jewish person in my school, and as it had in eighth grade, this provided my peers with ammunition to use against me. When the anti-Semitism began, I felt even more alone and isolated. It was as if no one truly had my back. Even my friends would take part and make hurtful comments. It got so bad that someone actually pasted a picture of Hitler on the outside of my locker.

I'll never forget the time I was taking a break from basketball practice to get some water from the fountain in the hall. I'd taken to wearing knee-high socks pulled all the way up as I'd seen professional basketball players do. As I drank from the fountain, I heard two kids having a conversation about me.

"Why does he wear those socks that way?" one asked.

The other replied, "Because he's a Jew."

It didn't even make any sense, but it hurt nonetheless. I felt different from everyone else in my school, and it seemed as if they were trying to rub that fact in my face whenever they could. The more meanness I experienced from others, the more desire I had to get even. I wasn't a fighter in the physical sense; as I've said, I was too afraid of the pain that would follow if I were to get in a fight. Not only that, but I was so sensitive and conscious of how I looked, that I couldn't possibly risk getting my face mangled by someone else's fists. So I continued to defend myself verbally instead. This got me into trouble on multiple occasions with my teachers and peers, and in one instance almost got me beat up. I'll never forget how I narrowly avoided the biggest fight of my life.

Apparently, in conversation with a friend, I'd called someone a very nasty name. Truth be told, I actually didn't remember doing this, but I was so angry in those days that a lot of things came out of my mouth that I wasn't necessarily conscious of. Since word travels fast in high school, this slanderous news made its way back to the guy who was never supposed to hear what I had to say. Suddenly I found myself in the midst of a very scary situation.

Toward the end of the day, one of the guy's friends came up to me and threw me against a locker. He said the only way we could settle this was to fight after school. I tried to brush off the whole encounter, but it really shook me up. I was terrified and didn't want the day to end. When the last bell rang, I rushed to my locker, grabbed my things, and headed for the exit—intending to go straight home. That's when I noticed that this person had come down to find me and was blocking the way out. Before I knew it, I was surrounded by a circle of people, and that circle slowly grew as word spread that there was about to be a fight. I tried to push my way out, desperate to get away, but they wouldn't let me pass.

The guy started yelling at me and pushing me hard, urging me to make the first move. But I refused. I told him that I was not going to hit him. If he wished, he could punch a defenseless person, but I would not fight back. I screamed this at the top of my lungs, furious that I was being coerced into something that I didn't want to be a part of. Luckily for me, he wasn't interested in beating me up if I wasn't going to participate. After he and his friends pushed me around some more and realized I really wasn't going to respond, they finally let me go.

That was the closest I ever came to being in a real fight. It was terrifying, and I was so grateful that I'd been able to walk away unscathed. But the really brutal part of that whole situation was that I was no longer only known as "the Jew," but also as the sissy who was afraid to fight. Still, that reputation was way better than having my face knocked in.

Unsurprisingly, however, my gratitude didn't last for long. I was angrier than ever, although I did my best to suppress it. I had no idea how to express my feelings in a healthy way, and I refused to use violence as my outlet. The school year came to an end just in time, and I eagerly escaped for the summer.

卐 回 卐

Summer camp was my happy place. Since I was very young, I'd spent most of my summers at an overnight camp that was about two hours from my home. For me, it was a magical place where I truly felt like myself, and the summer before eleventh grade was especially memorable.

You see, at camp I actually had a group of friends. We'd all known each other since we were young, although I'd started out as an outsider with them, too. All of the other kids lived in Ottawa and knew each other from school. I joined their group every summer, but wasn't part of their lives otherwise. Luckily, this all became less important as we got to know each other better, and true friendships began to flourish. By the time I'd reached my teens, I spent most of my year looking forward to camp, and this particular summer turned out to be far and away the best yet. I'd been longing to really fit in somewhere my whole life, and camp was the closest I'd ever come. For one, I was around other Jewish kids, so I automatically felt like I related to them on a deeper level. On top of that, I met people who'd had similar life experiences. The older we all got, the more I not only felt like a part of the group, but also a contributing member.

That summer was a huge boost to my self-esteem. I really got a chance to step into my greatness for the first time, and it felt awesome! It was as if I were liberated from the shackles that had been holding me back for years. I finally got the recognition and respect I was longing for. I received the Best Offensive Player award in the competitive flag-football game we played every summer, and I had the lead role in the camp musical. It was wonderful to finally be able to sing in front of other people. I was awarded Color War Captain, which is the highest honor for all counselors in training (CITs). I was actually popular. Girls liked me. And I started to feel really comfortable with myself. I got all that I'd been looking for in a span of seven weeks, but when the summer was over I was devastated. I didn't want these experiences to end, but I had to return home to Pembroke and go back to school.

※　回　※

When eleventh grade began, I decided to disengage from everyone. I was tired of holding back, not being able to express myself, not being able to defend myself, and not feeling like I belonged anywhere. This was difficult for me, because up to this point I'd always been engaged in some way. Now my anger was turning into sadness, and I dwelled in it until I became totally desolate and depressed. It was almost as if, as soon as I allowed all this negativity in, I wanted to feel it even deeper and with more intensity, because I'd never given myself the opportunity to have these real emotions before. The farther I fell into sorrow, the deeper I got caught up in the depression that I was experiencing. It was a downward spiral, and I wasn't able to stop it.

At school, my group of friends had changed multiple times, yet Steven remained the one constant. Although I didn't think I could fully trust anyone, he was the closest I had to a true friend. Still, I remember trying to describe how I was feeling to him while I was going through this depression, and I don't think he was at a point in his life where he could really understand or relate on any level. Based on his reaction, I decided that I couldn't share my issues with anyone, not even my parents. So I pretended that nothing had changed and kept everything to myself. At school I tried to remain focused in the classroom, because I didn't want to draw unwanted attention to myself. With the friends and acquaintances I did have, I still engaged in superficial conversations—never really letting them in, but trying to appear as normal as possible.

When it came to sports, I still played on as many teams as I could, but since I was now among the youngest members on the senior teams, I didn't get nearly as much playing time. It quickly began to seem as if I weren't really part of the team anymore, and I missed the physical outlet that playing had provided. I was lost in the one place where I had previously felt important.

I went home for lunch almost every day to avoid any additional interaction with people at school, and on weekends I'd stay in as much as possible. I occasionally went out for dinner with my parents, but most of the time I'd decline their offers and just stay on the couch. I watched a lot of movies that year, and our family dog, Brandy, actually became my best friend. I remember staying home alone, crying and talking to Brandy, feeling as if he were the only one I could open up to. I saw the love in his eyes, and it made me feel so grateful to at least have some type of companionship, even if he was a dog.

For most of the school year, I wished I lived closer to my camp friends. My parents had purchased a condo in Ottawa a few years prior, and fortunately we spent many weekends there. This gave me a chance to see those guys and escape life back home. I almost convinced my mom to let me to spend the year in the city, where I could go to high school with all my friends and live with my aunt. But this never actually happened, and I was more depressed as a result. Then my sadness started having an impact on the time I did spend in Ottawa. Every time I'd get together with my camp buddies, something would happen or someone would say something that would remind me that I was "the kid from Pembroke," the outsider. I'd spent years trying to be a full-time member of their group, someone they fully accepted, respected, and loved; but the reality was that I didn't live in their city, I didn't go to school with them, and, as a result, I was never truly one of them.

Throughout this entire year, no one really knew what I was going through, because I refused to open up. The heightened feelings of isolation drove me deeper into the hold of depression, and it became harder to free myself from it. When the summer rolled around, it was a breath of fresh air, and I returned to summer camp, this time as a tennis instructor.

Although this experience was not as fulfilling as the previous year, I still enjoyed myself, and it felt good to be in a position of leadership. Having responsibility for younger kids, both in my cabin and on the tennis court, taught me to become more aware of my actions and words and their impact on others. It allowed me to leave the depression and sadness of the previous year behind and look at the bigger picture for the first time.

Heading into twelfth grade, I saw the light at the end of the tunnel. If I got good enough grades, then I could get into a top university and finally leave all the drama behind. I'd never look back. I was clear on my goal for the year and made a promise to myself that, no matter what, I was getting into McGill University in Montreal and starting fresh—for real this time.

I had a renewed sense of purpose, as I now had something I was striving toward. These hopeful feelings helped lift the sadness and made school much more tolerable. I knew in my heart that this was going to be the last year I ever lived in this town, and it allowed me to open up to different people and actually accept them for who they were. I no longer dwelled on the fact that we didn't have much in common, that I didn't really trust any of them, or that I saw within each of them very little drive or motivation. Instead, I decided to participate in the social scene because I was tired of being miserable and wanted to have some fun. I engaged in superficial friendships with a group of guys, and although it was not satisfying on many levels, it did provide me with company and, for the most part, a short-term solution to the deep loneliness I'd felt throughout high school.

At the same time, I was working incredibly hard to boost my grades so that I could qualify for the bachelor of commerce program at McGill. This was no easy feat. Prior to my senior year, students in Ontario had been required to complete five years of school before going to college. Mine was the first class that would be expected to graduate in four years, meaning for one year there would be two classes of students graduating at the same time. This shift was part of a larger process of adjusting the curriculum to fit into four years. Because things were in flux, there was a lot of pressure on us to succeed. There was also heightened competition to get into university. As a result, the average grades necessary for acceptance to most colleges had risen by at least five percentage points.

This was a lot for 17-year-old me to handle. I was convinced that McGill was the school for me, and on some level I needed to get in to really prove to myself that I was worthy. Since it was one of the top schools in Canada, I needed my average to be close to 90 percent in order to be accepted. And up until this point, I'd never really put my greatest effort into my studies. I'd always been satisfied doing just enough work to get by. But now I needed to increase my average by 10 percent, and thus faced a lot of doubt as to whether I was smart enough to pull this off.

With my goal clearly defined, however, I moved past that doubt and put all my energy into achieving it. I was driven by the societal beliefs that motivate many high school students to go to university, which included: *If I don't get good grades, I won't get into a good university. If I don't get into a good university, I'll be closing a lot of doors on my future. If I want to be successful, I need to work hard and sacrifice everything else that gets in the way. Nothing good in life comes easy. If I don't get a good degree, I'll never be able to achieve all the things that I've been told will make life better and more enjoyable down the road.* The list went on and on.

Basically, somewhere along the line I'd come to believe that a college education was the key to a prosperous and happy life. As a result, my future rested on my ability to perform over the next few months, which increased my stress and anxiety. Despite all the drama and the fact that I was taking all of it way too seriously, I managed to succeed, and it felt really good. For the first time, my results in the classroom were fantastic. I boosted all my grades in the first semester, and my average was on par with getting accepted into McGill, just as I'd planned. However, what happened next was a complete curveball that I didn't see coming.

🔛 🔟 🔝

You see, I was so caught up in the web of negative thoughts I'd spun that I didn't have a clear perspective on what I was doing to myself or my body. About halfway through the school year, I began to experience some stomach issues. At first I thought nothing of it, because I'd grown up in a house where a nervous stomach was not only natural, but almost a given. I was told by both my brother and my father that I was experiencing the "Eisen gut," and it was just part of being in this family. It was genetic.

I had trouble believing this, though. How could my stomach be messed up because I was part of a particular family that I didn't even feel connected to at the time? As things got worse, however, I started to wonder if this was the case. I went to see doctors who did all sorts of tests and couldn't find anything clinically wrong with me, so they called it Irritable Bowel Syndrome (IBS). I didn't make the association at the time, but the harder I worked in school and the more pressure I put on myself to get higher grades, the worse my stomach pains got.

This is when I could have benefited from some of the insights I've since learned. For one, I now believe 100 percent that *your thoughts create your reality*. In order to grasp this idea better, it's important to first look at how your thoughts work. Most of what I was thinking at the time came from my unconscious mind. Things would simply pop up without me even realizing it. To understand what I mean, consider this: Have you ever been reading a book and suddenly your mind is elsewhere—imagining how your day will go tomorrow or where your next vacation will be? Does it ever seem strange to you that your mind is able to wander so far from the task at hand without you directing it there? That's the power of your subconscious.

Everything within your subconscious comes from an experience or thought you previously had. All that information is stored in your brain, often without you realizing it. When something happens, let's say a big test is announced in school, your subconscious kicks in and may create thoughts such as: *I'll never be able to pass this test, I'm not smart enough, There isn't enough time to study all this material,* or *I'm doomed.* Before you know it, you've created a story or scenario that seems very real to you. These thoughts then manifest themselves in the words you speak to others and to yourself. During this particular time, I was often overheard saying things like, "I'm totally going to fail," "I hate this teacher," and "Why did I even bother signing up for this class?"

What happens next is all these negative thoughts begin to create your actions. In my case, this meant pushing myself to study harder than I ever had before, all the while fearing I was going to fail. These actions eventually form your reality, and for me that was sickness.

Because I worked so hard and had the intellectual capacity to absorb the information I was studying, I was able to get the grades I needed—but they came at a cost. I was caught up in a vicious cycle of study, stress, fear, and illness. I worked hard, and my insides suffered as a result. My thoughts literally made me sick, to the point that it became a challenge at times to eat, drink, or sleep. Still, I refused to let my upset stomach get in the way of my goal. I kept working hard, and the high marks continued to come in. I pushed myself to the max. My mind was always active, and I had no idea how to slow it down.

I didn't listen to this first message my body gave me, so the second soon followed. A month into my second semester, I was told I had mononucleosis, or mono, a viral infection that can have serious repercussions if not treated with a lot of rest. The worst part about this was that I was no longer able to play any sports or partake in any physical activity. Being that I was only three games away from finishing my last year on the basketball team, and having just played the best game of my career, this was devastating. The bright side, however, was it appeared as though my mono wasn't such a severe case, and I was able to go to school and get all my homework done. It seemed that not even this illness could stop me from getting into college.

Thankfully, a few months later I got a letter indicating that I'd received early acceptance into the business program at McGill. I'd finally done it! At last I was able to take my foot off the gas and slow down a bit. But if you've ever tried to stop a car in motion, you know that it takes a lot of power. I was already so revved up that it was nearly impossible to stop now. I continued to push, and my stomach continued to cry out. When the mono had run its course, I was cleared to play sports again. While it would have been better to ease my way back into things, I jumped in head-first, determined to get back in shape as quickly as possible. So, unsurprisingly, less than a month later I sprained my ankle on the basketball court.

Obviously, my body was giving me some very clear signs, but I was totally blind to all of them. Instead of taking the cues to slow down, I started to feel sorry for myself, believing that life was working against me and the only way to beat it was to keep fighting and pushing. (All of this doubt and cynicism would become the foundation for my complete breakdown two years later.)

When the school year eventually came to an end, I graduated with a 93-percent average and finally began to see myself as smart and successful. I was on my way to Montreal, and I would continue to work hard to prove that I was worthy of getting into such a great school. This was my chance to start over. I was convinced, similar to my feelings heading into high school, that this time I was going to leave all my issues and challenges behind. I blamed the town I lived in for all my drama, heartbreak, and suffering. I assumed that going to college was the clean slate I needed.

Jeffrey's Story

Any parents reading this can surely identify with me when I say that the teenage years are not easy, for parents or kids. For me, though, parenting preteens and teens was actually easier, in some ways, than trying to decode the babble of babies or understand the frantic and illogical minds of children. I came to discover that I could relate much better to my kids at this stage in their lives. It's interesting that now, as I welcome grandchildren into the family, I feel so much more comfortable knowing that relating to infants and little ones is not my forte. Still, I'm probably more relaxed around my grandchildren than I ever was around our own kids when they were that age.

When Hailey, Allan, and Michael were growing up, my inability to connect made me feel extremely inadequate. But as they matured, I found it much easier to interact with them, and this made me feel a lot better about my role as a parent. As a result, the older my kids got, the more involved in their lives I became.

For one, I became the go-to parent when the children needed help with schoolwork. I actually enjoyed helping them with their assignments, and this was an area that I felt competent in. Plus, I figured that it was the least I could do, considering my wife did so much to run our household and organize the kids' activities. The only problem I had was that there never seemed to be enough time to give them my full attention. I'd come home from work just in time for dinner, and then after helping with homework, I'd still have a few hours of my own work to do. Luckily, in those days we didn't yet have smartphones, because I would have been even more distracted during family time than I already was.

You see, when you're in a hurry to accomplish so much, it's impossible not to always seem rushed and short on time. It's not how much time you actually have, but how you *feel* about that time. In my case, rushed, hurried, and under pressure were the feelings that seemed to come up most often, which meant that I was on edge for the majority of my life.

I always had a long list of goals that I wanted to accomplish, both in regard to my family and the business. Once I achieved all of them, I was confident my life would be better. It was all about getting to that elusive destination called "happiness." I figured that once I made enough money and the kids were at college and the business grew and so on . . . things would be better, and I'd be happier. I truly believed that when the stars finally aligned, my life would be good.

I remember working with a human-resources consultant who was helping make some changes in our company's organizational structure. He was helping my brother Robert (my business partner) and me understand what we each wanted from the business and what roles we wanted to play. After speaking with us individually, he came to the conclusion that I was a "destination focused" person and Robert was more "journey focused." In other words, I was always pushing hard to reach the finish line, and my brother was more interested in enjoying the road through life. At the time, I was really proud of myself for being driven toward the endgame. Little did I know that this very quality would cause so much pain and suffering that I'd finally have to give up my quest for the elusive holy grail.

One of the main problems with being so destination focused at that time was that it influenced the way I parented. I felt that it was my responsibility to teach our children how to plan for the future. Unfortunately, with an emphasis on the finish line comes a tendency to always be looking ahead and never appreciating what you have in the present moment. So while the children were still in high school, I encouraged them, especially the boys, to begin thinking about their careers. They were still young, but I thought they should be planning ahead to determine how they'd earn a living and support their families. I still believed it was the responsibility of the man to be the primary breadwinner of a family and to take care of the finances.

This may seem totally old-fashioned, and even sexist, but it's what I'd been taught growing up, and I'd never thought to question it. Like many parents, I took it upon myself to discuss with my children how important it was to start thinking about the ways in which they'd make money. While I did a lot of talking, I neglected to actually listen to my teenagers and find out what they thought was important or would make them happy. I believed that the only way to be happy was to be successful, and my definition of success included a good education, a good job, a spouse, a family, and enough money to live comfortably.

It wasn't until much later that I started to question these beliefs and redefine happiness. What I now know is that it's a state of mind, a feeling that exists in the present moment. It's not a big house, a lot of money, or a high-powered job. When we strive for these things, believing that happiness will come as a result, we often find ourselves disappointed when the goals are achieved but the joy never comes. Instead, we find ourselves reaching for the next accomplishment, wanting something more or bigger this time. Or if we do feel happiness, it's usually short-lived. The sense of elation wears off as we set out to slay the next dragon. I've come to realize now that my brother actually had the right idea; focusing on the journey can be far more gratifying and certainly less stressful.

If I could do this chapter of my life over again, I would not push so hard to cram my beliefs down my kids' throats. Rather, I'd focus on getting to know them and understanding their concerns, fears, and passions.

I remember an incident when my older two children came home from school very upset by how a teacher had handled a particular situation. They felt angry and frustrated that this person didn't understand the students and had done something that was unfair as a result. When they shared their feelings with me, I proceeded to defend their teacher and lectured them on the importance of respecting authority. Hailey and Allan went off to their rooms as angry and frustrated with me as they were with the teacher.

Luckily, Lois was more understanding than I'd been and went upstairs to talk with the kids. She was able to calm them down by listening to their side of the story, which was more than I was prepared to do. In the moment, I thought I was right and stood by the advice I'd given them. Looking back, though, I feel badly for the way I reacted. I'd been taught that people in positions of power are always right and should be respected no matter what. Obviously, these beliefs didn't serve me well when it came to helping my children deal with this situation. If only I'd been able to put aside what I thought and just listen empathetically to my kids, the whole blowup could have been avoided. I'd have earned their respect rather than demanding it.

Creating Perspective in the Family

Our family life could have been much more harmonious if we'd understood the concept of perspective. How could I have expected my children to see things the same way I did when they'd had fewer experiences? How could I have expected them to understand why I was always so cautious and concerned for their well-being when they weren't yet fully able to grasp that life could be dangerous? The reason we butted heads so often is because we were all stuck seeing things only from our own points of view, unwilling to budge. I didn't understand my kids, and they didn't understand me. Only now do I realize that it's unreasonable to expect others to accept or consider my perspective if I'm not willing to do the same for them. The truth is that the world isn't really "as it is," but as we see it, and we all see it differently.

To help you understand the idea of perspective, try imagining your life as a movie. Let's call it *My Life*. In this movie, you not only play the lead character, but you are also the writer, director, cinematographer, and producer. After all, this is your life.

Everyone else in your film is a secondary character and plays a supporting role, and some people play more important parts than others. Every character has a unique vantage point or perspective from which he or she sees the script, sets, cinematography—everything about it. However, since it's the movie of *your* life, you get to direct all aspects of each individual's performance. You get to tell the story of your life through your eyes only. You interpret every scene through the lens of your camera.

Now to complete this analogy, all of the secondary characters (your parents, kids, siblings, teachers, friends, and so on) have also created their own movies, each called *My Life*. They have the lead role in their own movies and work as producer, writer, and director. In each of their films, you act as a secondary character, and it's their turn to direct you. You can probably understand that the perspective you have as a character in someone else's story is very different from the one you have in your own. Hopefully this illustrates how complicated things can get when you interact with so many different people, all of them directing their own life movies, all at the same time.

Can you imagine watching one of your scenes where a particular event is playing out, while simultaneously watching the same scene in someone else's movie where you're in a supporting role? Anyone seeing these two take place at the same time would quickly realize that while they are both about the same event, they each interpret the situations and emotions in entirely different ways. No two movies will ever be the same, because no two perspectives are ever identical.

🔛 🔲 🔛

As a father, I wish I'd spent more time encouraging my kids to be themselves, rather than trying to improve what I thought were their weaknesses. I was always trying to "fix" them, to mold them into the people I wanted them to be. I think I did this because I was so heavily involved in the business world, where performance evaluations were critical. Although the evaluations had space for both strengths and weaknesses, in those days we spent much more time trying to correct what was wrong, rather than working with what was right. The belief was that if you rectified the weakness, the employee would be able to perform better. I took these practices very seriously and applied them to my children as well.

Over the years these practices have evolved in the workplace, and "weaknesses" were eventually replaced with "areas of improvement." Instead of telling employees how to change, we'd work together to come up with ways to improve. But even this didn't go far enough. While we all have strengths and weaknesses, I truly believe the focus should be on nurturing and expanding upon the strengths of each person—be it an employee or a child. Only when we focus on what we're good at are we able to find our passion.

Unfortunately, I didn't believe all of this when my wife and I were raising our kids, and instead made it my mission to help them improve on what we perceived to be their shortcomings. This proved to be a constant struggle. How can a father truly convince his teenagers that he knows best when his own life is full of stress, anxiety, and discomfort? How can he expect them to make changes when he's not prepared to do the same? It was these inconsistencies that made it very difficult for me to tell them, "Do as I say, not as I do."

But without being able to see the situation objectively, Lois and I continued to tell the children what to do, and they continued to ignore our advice, often arguing back. It made for a very challenging time for our family, and we were all filled with resentment, anger, and frustration. Although we still loved each other very much, we certainly didn't treat each other that way.

Now, I still don't believe that moms and dads should let their teenagers do whatever they want, but I know that the autocratic way of parenting didn't work well for us. Instead of creating a harmonious relationship with our kids, we put them on the defensive. Parenting teens is a fine balance, one that I was never able to perfect, although Hailey did tell us once that she appreciated the boundaries we set for her at this age. I believe it's the teenager's role to push back and move toward becoming more independent, while it's the parents' job to lay down, wherever possible, mutually acceptable boundaries.

All societies demand a certain appropriateness when it comes to the behavior of their citizens. In order to ensure that people do the right things, laws and consequences are created. The same holds true in families. But the trick, as I see it, is to encourage appropriate behavior by helping your children understand the repercussions of their actions rather than autocratically demanding that they act a certain way. Still, no matter how hard you work as a parent to pass on these lessons, sometimes the only way for kids to learn is from experience.

I remember when Michael was taught a hard lesson about consequences. He was on a school ski trip, and on the way to the hill, the students were told not to drink anything on the bus, not even water. Michael was the kind of teenager who believed that if a rule didn't make sense, he shouldn't have to follow it. While this kind of tenacity has come in handy for him as an adult—helping him push beyond societal expectations and carve out his own version of success—it didn't serve him well as a teen. He decided to open a bottle of soda and drink it on the bus, because he was thirsty and it didn't make sense not to. As a result, he and a few other kids who joined him in breaking this rule were suspended from school for three days. While other parents stepped in to appeal this ruling, we decided to let the punishment stand. Michael wasn't happy with us, feeling as if we'd deserted him in a time of need. But we believed this was an important lesson that he had to learn. Since then, Michael has continued to fight hard against things he doesn't believe in, but has managed to do so within the confines of the law.

಄   ಄   ಄

Now that my kids are adults, I've begun to realize just how influential some of my own practices and beliefs were on their lives, especially regarding fear. I'm one of the baby boomers, born to the generation who fought to defend democracy in World War II. We lived through the Cuban Missile Crisis, when the possibility of nuclear war seemed very real. We lived through the 1960s—an era of anarchy and civil disobedience. So it's no wonder then that we all felt so fearful. But sadly, we took these emotions and handed them directly to our children without realizing the effects they'd have. Although I grew up consumed by fear, it wasn't until much later that I realized how debilitating and disempowering this was. I believe we're facing an epidemic of fear in our society today, and this is preventing us from achieving peace: within and without.

Fear: Real or Imagined?

Fear isn't always bad. It does have a purpose and can be useful when the threat we're experiencing is real, as it stimulates the necessary adrenaline to propel us into action in dangerous situations. But since so much fear comes from imagined peril, it can become extremely disempowering rather than beneficial.

In earlier civilizations, fear was one of the keys to survival. With only basic tools for protection, humans relied on their own abilities to flee when their lives were at risk. The fight-or-flight response, which is triggered by fear, produces adrenaline that helps humans run faster, fight harder, and escape danger. In the past this was instinctual—our thoughts and emotions were aligned with the present moment. But somewhere in our evolution, fear shifted from being essential to our existence to extremely debilitating. As societal structures were built to look after our immediate safety—emergency services, police, well-constructed buildings, locked doors, and so on—our fear was transferred to future happenings or imagined danger. Today it's considered a negative emotion that prevents us from succeeding, and even causes sickness in our bodies. Most of us don't want to feel afraid but often aren't sure how to shake this response.

When the feelings of fear are based on something imagined, the adrenaline that's produced creates a sense of discomfort—rapid heartbeat, sweaty palms, and stomach-ache, for example. Since what we're afraid of isn't real, we're unable to take the action necessary to escape it, and thus the chemicals created to propel us into action begin to debilitate us. What we experience are feelings of agitation, anxiety, and discomfort. Instead of reacting, we try to address the fear in our minds, which often creates an endless loop of thoughts that keep us focused on a hypothetical situation that may actually never occur. The more we focus on the fear, the more helpless we feel.

It's difficult to say for sure how the dread of future events became so prevalent in humans. Perhaps as our world became more complex, people began to feel intimidated by what they didn't understand. As the pace of life began to quicken, and change happened at such a rapid rate, many individuals no longer felt as if they could keep up or remain in the present moment. The fear of the unknown has been around for a long time, but the more intricate and complicated life gets, the scarier it becomes. I believe that the human desire to be in control, coupled with our inability to predict the future, has intensified fear overall.

In order to protect our offspring and loved ones, we share our apprehensions with them and pass along all the associated negative emotions. If you're a parent, then I'm sure you can identify with this. When was the last time you expressed one of your fears to your children? Many of us have told them not to drive at night, to stay away from large crowds, to only travel to safe destinations, and to never talk to strangers. How often have we instilled anxieties in our children that have made them so afraid that they lose the courage to be themselves? I know that I did this, and I'm still trying to undo the impact that it's had on their lives.

If I was granted a do over of my kids' teenage years, I'd have gone about things differently. Instead of raising them to fear failure, I would have shown them how to embrace it and the lessons that come with it. Instead of bringing them up to be scared of getting sick, I would have taught them that they have the power to heal themselves. I'd still want them to be cautious and discerning, but not slaves to fear.

While parenting was getting a bit easier for me, the year 2000 brought with it many new stresses. You know the saying, "It never rains but it pours"? Well, that year it started to pour, and before I knew it, I was soaked. My Crohn's disease, which had been in remission for some time, began to act up again, and I experienced regular attacks that were extremely painful. I also started to have severe pain in my lower back and was diagnosed with a herniated disc. In addition to my health issues, Allan became very sick and was diagnosed with ulcerative colitis, but his doctors were unsure if the medication used to treat this disease would be powerful enough to get his raging symptoms under control.

A few months earlier, our daughter Hailey left home for university and Lois was forced to deal with the absence of the only other female member of our household. It is an emotionally trying time for a mother when she sees her children leave the nest and begin to fly on their own, and this was even more intense because Hailey was our only daughter and she and Lois were extremely close.

Meanwhile, the economy was plummeting and business was getting increasingly stressful. Not only were we unsure if we'd make enough money to keep the company afloat, but my relationship with my brother was beginning to unravel. Things were not going as planned, and I felt as if I had very little control over anything.

Michael was at a stage where he had shut down a lot of his communication with us and was going through his own internal struggle. As parents we felt extremely guilty and bewildered, and we racked our brains trying to figure out what we'd done to create this situation. Needless to say, with all the strain that everyone in the family was feeling, the tension was palpable. We're all extremely vocal, so we expressed our frustration with harsh words and raised voices.

What I didn't realize at the time is that when stress and pressure become so severe, the ability to come up with viable solutions gets increasingly difficult. That's why so many people end up hitting rock bottom before they begin to make significant changes in their lives. Well, I was quickly approaching the bottom, and looking back, I wish I hadn't waited so long to make different choices. I wish I hadn't put myself through so much discomfort before I took action. I wish I'd sought out support and guidance much earlier, before things were really blown apart. The truth is, you don't have to wait until you're at the bottom before you start climbing back to the top—you just have to be self-aware enough to stop yourself midfall.

That's one of the reasons why Michael and I are writing this book. In sharing my mistakes with you, I'm hoping you'll look more compassionately upon your own life and realize that help does exist and a better life is possible. The more people who join us on the journey of awakening, the better the world will be.

Chapter Four

FROM BREAKDOWN TO BREAKTHROUGH

Jeffrey's Story

If I had to identify one period of my life when things really felt out of my control, it would have to be around the time that Allan finished his second year of college and his ulcerative colitis worsened. It was apparent that the medication he was on wasn't working, and the only solution was to have his entire colon surgically removed. When a child goes through a traumatic experience, parents often feel the pain as their own. I remember the anguish Lois and I tried to suppress as we supported Allan through this terrifying time. The surgery he was about to undergo would not only involve a long recovery period, but it would also have life-changing repercussions. He was braver than I could have ever imagined him to be, but we all felt a huge amount of fear going into this experience.

I'll never forget standing at the door of the recovery room with Lois, looking in on Allan after his surgery. The mixed feelings of fear and hope made it one of the most trying times in our lives. All of this helped me put my own life in perspective, and I began to realize that some of the things I thought were so important were actually totally insignificant. It's interesting how when you stare deep into your mortality, the things that are important to you change. I realized I really needed to make some changes in my life—but first my priority was Allan's recovery.

At the same time, Michael was beginning his freshman year at McGill, and we needed to move him into his residence. So I decided to stay with Allan at the hospital as he began his long road to recovery, and Lois and Hailey took Michael to Montreal to help him move in. It must have been difficult for all of our kids, as they were trying to adapt to the changes around them amidst so much uncertainty.

Likely due to all the stress and anxiety I felt around Allan's illness, my Crohn's, which had already been acting up, continued to worsen. I met with my doctor while Allan was still in the hospital, and he recommended that I have my ileum, a section of my inflamed small intestine, removed immediately. It had come to the point where surgery was my only option, and the timing was awful. I can only imagine how emotionally exhausting all of this must have been for Lois. I literally moved into Allan's hospital room as he was being released, and preparations were made for my own procedure. With two of our kids at university and Allan and me at home recovering, it was not an easy time for our family. But we survived. And as the saying goes, what doesn't kill you makes you stronger.

▨ ▣ ▨

A year prior to all of this, around the time I turned 50, I began to sense that something was missing in my life. Although I wasn't feeling the urge to shave my head or buy a convertible as some do when they reach midlife, I did feel the need to make some sort of drastic change. That being said, I had no idea what it would be or how it would come about.

I'd accomplished so much in my professional and personal life. I had a wonderful family, and although we all had our moments, we loved each other unconditionally. While the business had its financial challenges, it had done well overall. We'd successfully grown the small company that my father started in 1946 into a multimillion-dollar enterprise. This afforded us the monetary resources to have a beautiful home, a pool in the backyard, and great family vacations where we were able to show the kids more of the world than the small town they grew up in.

Lois and I were happy together for the most part. Even though we too faced ups and downs, they were nothing we couldn't handle together. We'd decided early in our marriage that it was important for us to have getaways, just the two of us. Even when the children were small, we made an effort to arrange for babysitters so that we could have our own time together. As the kids left for college, we began to reconnect as a couple. Becoming empty nesters gave us the chance to pick up where we had left off in developing our relationship.

I'd also accomplished a great deal personally by getting involved in our community as the president of the local Rotary Club, as I mentioned earlier, as well as becoming an effective leader at work. I felt that I'd done very well considering I hadn't finished my university degree, hadn't worked for anyone expect my father, and was largely self-taught in how to manage and run a business. Looking back, I was at a place many people only dream of getting to. But I was perplexed: *So now what? Is this all my life is meant to be? Is it simply about striving to get ahead and then learning to cope when things don't go my way? Is it about spending part of the time feeling like I'm on top of the world and the rest of the time hovering around the bottom? Is this all I have to look forward to for the rest of my life?*

I knew that I should be happy, but something important was missing. I felt discontentment, dissatisfaction, unhappiness, and restlessness. Believe it or not, it was from this place of desperation that the answers came to me—and they turned up in a rather magical way. But it wasn't until after Allan and I had recovered from our respective surgeries that any of this actually started to take shape.

As life went back to normal, I was tempted to waver from my commitment to seek out change. I told myself, *Maybe things are okay the way they are. Maybe I shouldn't rock the boat. What if I go looking for something more and can't find it?* Luckily, the discipline and drive that had gotten me into my current situation served me well, and I pushed past these doubts, determined to do something different. I didn't really know what to do, but I knew the life I was living wasn't what I wanted anymore. I guess I've always had a deep underlying optimism, or maybe it was a naïveté that things would work out, so moving forward on this new journey wasn't as frightening as it could have been.

I started by making some pretty major decisions that I knew would force me to dive right into change. Lois and I decided that we would move from our home in Pembroke to Ottawa, Canada's capital and a much larger city about 90 minutes away. This was relatively easy because, as Michael mentioned earlier, we already owned a condo there that we'd purchased several years prior. At that time, we'd discussed buying a cottage and had concluded that since we already lived in a rural setting, we'd rather have a second home in the city where we could enjoy culture, shopping, and nightlife. So we'd invested in a beautiful place on the Rideau Canal in downtown Ottawa and spent many weekends and holidays there with our family. The fact that we already had our home and loved it made the decision to sell our house in Pembroke easier. The business had a facility in Ottawa, too, so I could work from that office and travel to Pembroke when it was required.

The other major decision I made around the same time was to hire a management team to take on the responsibility of running the day-to-day affairs of our company. I knew that I had to do something to take pressure off myself or else my physical, mental, and emotional well-being would continue to pay the price. The long road of stepping back from my very active role in the business was full of great learning opportunities.

These two major decisions were the catalysts that started me on my path to self-discovery. Through this journey, I've discovered my true identity and learned to feel more comfortable in my own skin. I've been able to reexamine the conditioned beliefs handed down to me from my parents and teachers and let many of those ideas go, replacing them with new values and beliefs. I've hit many bumps along the way that have forced me to wake up and become more conscious about my life and the choices I was making.

I know that many people are afraid to embark on their own journeys because they don't feel comfortable with attempting a transformation. The fear of the unknown has prevented so many individuals from embarking on this path. What I realized is that if I wanted my life to shift for the better, I was going to have to embrace change. The path I was on wasn't making me happy, and so I was going to have to take a huge chance and trust that somehow things would work out. Upon realizing this, I pushed my fears aside and focused on taking steps to make my life better.

Making Friends with Fear

The first and most important step in overcoming your fear is becoming aware of what your fears are and making friends with them. Learning to slow down your thoughts and actually listen to what's going on in your head is the first step in achieving this awareness. Once your mind is moving at a more manageable pace, it will become much easier to pick out your apprehensions when they come up.

Later in my life when I worked with one of my many coaches, I learned a simple practice that really helped me identify my fears. I'd listen carefully to my thoughts all day long, and as soon as a fear thought surfaced (for example, *What if the business doesn't make enough money this quarter?* or *What if we run into trouble?*), I'd catch myself and say out loud, "Fear!" I was actually surprised at first by how many times I was saying this word each day. My mind was full of fear, and I hadn't even realized it.

Both Michael and I strongly believe that awareness can lead to choice, and making the right choices can actually change how we see and live our lives. The more aware I became of my fears, the more I realized that I had a choice to either dwell on and resist these thoughts or accept, change, and let go of them. Even today, no matter how strongly I believe that I should only be focusing on the now, my mind still has a tendency to wander. The key, I've discovered, is to find something more empowering—like faith or trust—to replace the negative thoughts. By simply affirming that things will work out well, no matter how challenging or difficult they appear to be, I've been able to let go of so many of my fears.

Some people may say that it's naïve to think things will always work out for the best. They could be right, but I know that it's better to be naïve and happy than afraid and miserable. If we're unable to accurately predict how the future will unfold anyway, then what difference does it make if we decide to believe that all will work out well or if calamity will forever be our nemesis? Is an outcome going to be adversely affected by having a positive view of how things will turn out, even if this perspective is based solely on faith and trust? Will our reality be any different if our thoughts about the future are full of fear or full of faith? I guess that depends on what we believe.

There are people like Michael and me who believe that thoughts create reality—in which case, the positive thoughts are more likely to lead to a happy life than the fear-based thoughts. But even if you don't believe this to be true, why not choose thoughts that make you experience joy rather than ones that cause you to feel depressed? It's really that simple.

We believe that fear thoughts are sticky and dark and don't feel very good. On the other hand, images of faith and hope are fluffy and light. So even if you don't accept that your thoughts have any influence on your outcome, why would you ever choose something that brings up a distressing emotion? Why would you decide to punish yourself with doubt and apprehension, which are based only on a supposition about the future anyway? Why not concentrate on love and trust, which at least make you feel more hopeful about a future situation? If you do believe that your thoughts create your reality, then you will definitely want to replace fearful thoughts with positive ones, because those very thoughts will bring you what you're looking for. If you want to be a happier, more relaxed person, then consider switching your focus from fear to faith, and watch how different your life becomes.

Around the time I turned 52, a number of events in my life aligned, guiding me further on the path of change. I have come to understand that there's a lot more to coincidences than just random individuals and events appearing at opportune times. In fact, I believe that there's a power much greater than I can sometimes fathom, guiding certain things to happen. Changes occur when we're prepared to follow them.

Dave, the human-resources consultant who was working with our company, had become a friend and confidant. He shared with me many concepts about leadership, management, and people in general. Little did I know that my great interest in these subjects would lead to me discovering my true passion in life: working with and understanding people. Dave and I began to do work on creating a new culture for the business, one of empowerment. Around that time, Lois and I were preparing for a vacation in Florida, and Dave recommended a new book he'd just read that he thought I might enjoy. It turned out that this very book, *The Monk Who Sold His Ferrari* by Robin Sharma, would be the magical key to unlock so many doors for me.

I've now come to appreciate the moments in my life where serendipitous events open up a multitude of possibilities that I never imagined. This has led me to let go of my controlling nature and just go with the flow, eager to see where new experiences or adventures might take me. Letting go has allowed my life to be much more full and exciting than it ever was when I tried to be in command of every decision and experience. I'm not sure if it was the information in Robin Sharma's book, the fact that I was on vacation, or that I was so ready for this awakening, but after reading *The Monk Who Sold His Ferrari* in record time, I went to a bookstore in Florida and purchased three more titles by the same author. I was fascinated by what he wrote about, and it opened me up to an entirely new world of beliefs.

Upon returning home, I researched the author online and found that he was hosting a weekend-intensive workshop in Toronto called "Awakening the Best Self." I was convinced that I had to attend this event to learn more about these ideas and principles. And I wanted to share all of this with the important people in my life, so I bought tickets for myself, Lois, Hailey, and Allan (Michael was on a trip to Israel at the time). I also invited one of our top managers from work who was interested in this kind of thing to join us. So we all went to Toronto and participated in what would become a life-changing event. It was an extremely intense and emotional few days, and I had the chance to search deep within myself for the first time ever. I was forced to look long and hard at my feelings and my fears.

I'd found out that Robin Sharma had a program he called "The Master Series," where he worked with top executives for a one-year period, coaching them in business and life. It was my intention, going into this weekend workshop, to become one of Robin's coaching clients—although the possibility of this actually happening seemed unlikely. I'll never forget approaching him at one of the breaks and expressing my desire to work with him. It turned out that particular program wasn't affordable for me at the time, but Robin made an exception and agreed to work with me for three months. I was now totally committed to this journey; there was no turning back. It seemed as though some magical power really wanted me to move forward, and all I had to do was have the courage to follow along the yellow brick road. I had absolutely no idea where this all would lead, but I was willing to give it a try.

I have come to realize how important it is sometimes to let go of your fears, give up your desire to be in control, and simply follow the opportunities that open up before you. Looking back on this time, it seems that's exactly what I did, and it has definitely paid off. Little did I know that I was about to uncover my true passion.

圖　回　圆

I was so excited to start learning with Robin. Although at times I felt a bit nervous about what was unfolding, there seemed to be a deeper knowing that I was on the right path. I began to understand much about myself and how to become a better leader for our company.

Robin had been a high-profile lawyer who discovered, like so many of us, that his profession was not his passion. He went on his own journey of self-discovery and found a whole new life as an author, speaker, and coach. He had a great desire to share his knowledge with others, and I was now going to be the recipient of it all. After coming to Ottawa and spending a full day with me, seeing our company's facilities, and even talking with my wife, Robin and I began our learning together.

The program was fairly structured, and I started by reading some of the books he recommended. What ensued was a systematic unraveling of my belief systems and an introduction to a whole new set of possibilities. I started to understand that everything on the planet is made up of energy vibrations. When we're feeling joy, we vibrate at a higher frequency; and when we're sad, angry, or fearful, our vibration is lower. I explored how what I did, what I said, and where I went impacted my energy levels.

I remember very distinctly when I realized for the first time that watching and reading the news was not serving me well. Why was I spending so much time focusing on what was wrong in the world, getting worked up with fear about the issues and catastrophes I had no control over? While being aware of what's going on is extremely important, watching the news wasn't doing me or the world any good.

I began to examine most of my routines and habits, and developed new ones that felt better. One of my first new practices was waking up early every morning. I'd always struggled with the fear of not getting enough sleep. Perhaps this came from those years when the kids woke up in the night and I'd have trouble getting back to sleep, thus feeling exhausted at work the next day. With a belief that the more sleep I got, the better, you can imagine how I first resisted the concept of rising at 5:00 A.M. to begin a morning ritual that I can now honestly say has totally changed my life.

Each morning when I woke at five, I'd begin the practices of journaling, meditating, reflecting, and exercising. At first, meditating was extremely challenging. I had a very busy mind, and I was of the belief that my brain is one of my greatest assets. While I now realize that this is true, I discovered that we're meant to be more in balance with our thoughts and feelings, rather than operating only from our heads.

I can still recall my first attempt at meditation. There I sat in my dark office with nothing but complete silence. Have you ever tried to *watch* your thoughts? As soon as I sat down with the intention of being silent—with no music, distractions, or reading—my inner voice went wild: *What are you doing? This is crazy. Imagine what they'd think if they saw you sitting here. Come on, just turn on the computer and get to work.*

Years later, I'm now able to meditate with ease, and I love the quiet time it allows me. Even when the world is bustling all around me, I can quiet my mind and be in the moment. When I first experienced the state of inner peace from this exercise, I was totally amazed. I continued to try out various methods and found guided meditations to be what worked best for me. I developed a practice of sitting for 20 minutes every morning and 20 minutes every evening. This has served me well. So much so that a few years ago, with the assistance of a great singer and composer, I created my own audio program with guided meditations and music. (See *Meditation* in the Resources section.)

Journaling was also very interesting and healing for me. In the beginning, I'd just write whatever came into my head. It was an ideal way to empty my busy mind. Over time, it also allowed me to put to paper some of the things that had been bothering me for years. I was able to work through a lot of the feelings, many of them not so good, that I'd had about my family. Writing from your heart can be a therapeutic way of working through things that have been locked up inside. I've come to understand how important it is to express these stored emotions. When I was younger, I tried hard to repress everything, not wanting anyone to see what I thought were my weaknesses. Finally, I was realizing how great it felt to give voice to them, to express them and then let them go. (See *Writing or Journaling* in the Resources section.)

Exercise was also an important part of my routine. After all, what good was it to be feeling emotionally fit if my body was still hurting? I hired a personal trainer and began to get myself into better shape. I allowed myself regular massages and began to treat my body with the respect and care it deserved. It responded well, giving me better health and increased energy.

I'd always had a great sense of dedication and discipline, and I was beginning to use it in a very positive way. I began to read fervently, taking in all this new knowledge about how to live a calmer, more peaceful, and purpose-centered life. Robin taught me so many new behaviors—for example, using my car as a "university on wheels." Instead of having the radio on when I was driving, I listened to self-empowering audio programs. I also learned how important it is to focus on what's going well for me as opposed to what's going wrong. Choosing this positive route made a huge difference in my professional and personal lives.

Robin instructed me to do something he called the "Weekly Design System." It consisted of a weekly report that I wrote, telling my story for the past seven days and reflecting on my thoughts and experiences. I then recorded my week's truly exceptional moments, allowing me to learn the art of celebration. After that, I'd rate my week by giving it a score between one and ten, creating a sense of measurement for my progress. The last part of the report was to set the intention for the coming week's truly exceptional moments, giving me the chance to focus on the change I wanted to incorporate.

Around the same time, I also started keeping track of the number of books I read and the number of audio programs I listened to. I was amazed by how many books I could get through in a year, especially because I'd never been an avid reader. The learning continued, but one of the most important aspects of my "education" was to walk my talk.

I've realized that true wisdom is applied knowledge, so putting all of this new information into practice was critical in changing my life. I created a vision of what I wanted my life to be, discovered my purpose, and firmed up the values I desired to live by and what my future should look like. This became my guide for the life I was trying to manifest. I was finally becoming more conscious about what was going on for me and how I wanted it to play out. Reflecting on my initial life vision as I write this chapter, I realize that I've accomplished a great deal of what I set out to. I can honestly say that I've successfully lived up to the future story I wrote for myself all those years ago.

Today, things continue to unfold for me in all their glory as I keep learning and growing and sharing with others the knowledge I've gained. Even though I was doing all this work on myself, I still faced many challenges at work and in my personal life. But I was also figuring out how to handle situations in a much more effective and less stressful way. It was good to be on this journey, as I was understanding much about myself and the ways of the world. Little did I know then that what I was doing would not be a short-term corrective action, but a new way of life.

Michael's Story

I began a new phase of my life in the fall of 2003, one that was supposed to bring me all the happiness, belonging, self-worth, and optimism that had been lacking for the past 18 years. It was my fresh start, and there was no looking back—literally. I thought that the easiest way to leave all the suffering behind was to forget that it ever happened. I decided that moving to a new city was my big opportunity to meet people who had no idea who I was. Therefore, I made every effort possible to ensure that very few knew the truth about my past.

I was as petrified as I was excited for this opportunity, because my track record of meeting new people hadn't been the greatest up until this point. I vividly remember the night before I moved into my dormitory. I bawled my eyes out in the hotel room with my mom and sister, who'd come along to Montreal to help me move. However, the tears quickly turned to joy the next morning when I met new friends within the first few hours of arriving at McGill. What made the transition easier was that everyone was in the same boat, facing the same fears and challenges of moving away from home for the first time. This allowed me to feel at ease, because on some level I already fit in and was connected to so many other students through this common experience.

And so I was off and running. The first week of school was Frosh Week, during which we were encouraged to participate in activities and attend parties, all with the focus of meeting new people from the various residences. There were so many students from different cities and countries, all looking to make new friends. What a wonderful chance this was for me to get acquainted with individuals from all over the world and finally live in a city that was full of culture and opportunities.

Since at the time I blamed most of my difficulties in high school on the town that I grew up in, I decided that I never wanted to be associated with Pembroke again. So when I met new people, I'd tell them that I was from Ottawa. And because my parents had moved there that year, I figured that I wasn't telling a complete lie. The only glitch was that there were a few individuals at McGill with me who were actually from Ottawa. Although we hadn't known each other that well, they did know that I was from Pembroke. This created some anxiety for me, because I always worried that my new friends would find out that I hadn't been totally honest. To this day, there are still some friends I made at college who have no idea that I grew up in Pembroke. I never wanted to be labeled as "the small-town kid"; I'd had enough of being different and an outsider. So I stuck to the story of coming from Ottawa, and it worked out well. Except for a few minor issues here and there, for the most part I was truly able to create a new beginning for myself.

Meeting new people became my favorite thing to do. I felt like a kid in a candy store—there were so many options to choose from. I made sure I belonged to many different groups, because I wanted to make up for lost time. I was having so much fun socializing that the whole academic part of school was pushed to the background for the time being. I needed this opportunity to really break free from the limitations I'd put on myself, and I was finally gaining confidence and starting to discover a little bit about who I truly was.

▨ ▣ ▨

During this time, my love for sports blossomed even more, and at McGill there was always an opportunity to play. They had intramural teams for everything, and the facilities I had access to were what I'd dreamed of all through high school. I enrolled in as many activities as possible: flag football, basketball, soccer, and inner-tube water polo. I'd also swim and work out in the gym. It was all so much fun, and everybody kept saying that in the first year your grades don't matter, so I bought into that belief and focused on having a blast.

Life was a big party. Every night of the week, everyone would go to a bar or club. At the time I was 18, the legal drinking age in Quebec, and since my stomach was now feeling much better because I wasn't stressed, I reasoned that I had a lot of catching up to do. For the first time in a while, I was relatively healthy. And so

I drank. Alcohol became a crutch that I used to transform myself into the person I wanted to be. It was as if every time I drank, I was able to forget about all those silly worries and beliefs that were holding me back.

This was the year that my experience with girls began to change as well. Throughout high school, I had the tendency to fall in love way too easily. On some level I believe I was longing for someone to care for me in return. I was in love with wanting to be loved. There were countless times that I'd fall for girls who were my friends. I had these deep feelings but, for the most part, I wasn't brave enough to tell them how I felt.

As high school progressed and these feelings got stronger, I decided I could no longer hold them in anymore. From that point on, I decided to express my love anytime I felt it. Unfortunately for me, it was never reciprocated. Most of these girls didn't see me as more than just a friend. As a result, I'd already had my heart broken many times when I arrived on campus. But once I was there, I started to question whether I really wanted to feel this way at all. I thought, *If this is what love feels like, then I don't want any part of it.* I began to subscribe to what many of my guy friends were doing at the time—basing relationships with girls purely on the physical connection and not allowing emotions to get involved.

I found that through drinking and partying I was able to close off my emotions quite easily. Alcohol also made me feel as though I had nothing to lose and gave me the courage to talk to anyone. As a result, I met a lot of new girls and had many new experiences. It was fun at the time, but it all caught up with me eventually, and then I had four years of unprocessed emotions to work through as a result. Looking back, I can see that I needed those experiences to help me realize what my true values were and how I wanted my life to be going forward.

Socially, this was the best year of my university life. As I've described, I finally came out of my shell and began to express myself freely, make friends easily, and engage in conversations I'd never had the courage to be a part of before. But I was still stuck with the belief that I had to impress everyone I met and that their opinions of me would shape our relationship. While I was finally discovering aspects of myself that were more genuine, I still had a long way to go before I was able to truly live in my *authentic self.*

On the Road to Authentic Living

One of the greatest obstacles to finding your authentic self and having the courage to live in a genuine way is the belief that the opinions of others actually matter. Throughout the first 19 years of my life, my desire to be accepted, liked, and even loved by others made it very difficult for me to ignore these points of view. So many of us have lost our connection to what feels right because we've sentenced ourselves to trying to please others. Only when we are able to truly stop caring what people think and start behaving in a way that feels good will we be able to, as the famous quote that's been frequently attributed to Mark Twain goes, "Sing like no one's listening, love like you've never been hurt, dance like nobody's watching, and live like it's heaven on earth."

Another common obstacle to authentic living is the fear of being vulnerable. The word is defined as "capable of being physically or emotionally wounded." It has a negative connotation, which is why many people are afraid to be vulnerable. But what if this wasn't a bad thing? What if this openness to whatever comes your way—hurt, joy, pain, or pleasure—was the only way to discover your true self? If you get hurt, at least you know what causes you pain and that you're able to cope with it. If you're shamed, at least you know what shames you and can adapt as a result.

Embracing all of yourself is the only way you'll be able to connect with your true self. When you resist your vulnerability, you prevent yourself from having any authentic experiences—in essence, you stop feeling and live completely through your head. It's important to remember that feelings are the guidance you'll need in order to live authentically. Vulnerability is not just opening yourself up to disappointment; it's also opening yourself up to love. You'll never truly receive love in your life until you allow yourself to be vulnerable.

We are made up of all sorts of characteristics and qualities. Where there is happiness, there is also sadness; where there is love, there is also fear; where there is truth, there is also falsehood. If we embrace the fact that we are everything, then we'll be able to see our world in a different light. In order to truly live in our greatness, we need to admit our so-called weaknesses along with our strengths. In order to live in our light, we need to acknowledge our darkness. Being truly authentic is accepting all parts of ourselves. The more we come to love ourselves wholly and completely, the more we can have an authentic and conscious life.

As my freshman year progressed, I was living the good life and was happy. But the class work started to catch up with me. Up until this point, I'd believed that as long as I put in hard work, I would always come out with good grades. Throughout my first year at school, my efforts came in waves. The way the schedule was set up, there were four times during the school year when everything got super busy and students put their social lives on hold to focus solely on studying. Just as I was trying on many different personalities and going through the process of figuring out who I was, so too was I exploring a variety of styles when it came to studying.

I came into college thinking that I was one of the smart kids, so I figured I could mimic what those individuals were doing in terms of studying and I'd be fine. This meant that I'd slack off for the first five weeks, and then when midterms came around I'd get serious and work as hard as I could. Well, during my very first set of midterms I had a taste of what university was all about. I had five exams in October, and the first was sociology. I got 53 percent. Needless to say, I hadn't really paid attention throughout much of this class and had relied on the textbook to study for the test. That tactic hadn't worked at all. My other grades were quite average, and I was okay with that.

For the second half of the semester, I figured out a way to boost my sociology grade. I was told that I must actually attend Friday tutorials and that I needed to go to one specific tutorial leader. She was really nice and provided us with questions ahead of time to prep for the exam. This changed everything, and I brought my mark up to a B+ by the end of the semester.

For most of my first year, I'd borrow notes from my friends, find past exams to study from, and put in just enough effort to get by with slightly below-average grades. Throughout this whole time, I believed that my grade point average (GPA) was not cumulative and that my first-year grades didn't count toward my overall score. This is what someone had told me, and I believed it wholeheartedly.

In my second semester, I faced a bigger challenge, as I saw a lot of people around me skipping classes. Thinking that I was just as smart as they were, I figured I could also play hooky and teach myself the material by reading the textbook. I figured I'd need about two weeks to learn all of the information before an exam. So I tried this with one of my most boring classes. I learned the hard way that this was not the most effective way for me to study, and I almost failed that course, plus one other class, and my GPA going into the second year was 2.94 out of a possible 4.0. It was only then that I found out my GPA *was* actually cumulative over four years, and I'd be facing an uphill battle to make up for the poor academic results I'd gotten as a freshman. Still, I hoped that since I'd put very little effort into the first year, I should be able to turn my marks around, as long as I just worked harder.

🕮 🔲 🕮

When the second year began, I noticed many of my old belief systems start to bubble up. These included: *If I don't get good grades, then I won't get a good job, have a successful life, or get any of the things that will bring me happiness.* I was also convinced that, *The harder I work, the more I'll succeed.* My freshman GPA made me question my ability to do well in school. I felt ashamed that I'd done so poorly, and so I began my sophomore year with the belief that I was going to have to work my butt off to make sure I could turn it around. I put an enormous amount of pressure on myself compared to my peers and constantly strove for better results.

The bachelor of commerce program I was in was quite competitive, and everyone was trying to come out on top. The prize, we thought, was getting the best job upon graduation. I bought into this belief, and I studied to compete and get good grades. I had to prove my worth all over again: that I was worthy of going to McGill University and the future jobs and opportunities that would come my way. I put so much pressure on myself that every exam, every grade, every project felt as if I had my whole life riding on it, with everything to lose if it didn't go the way I planned. And so, I slowly transformed from carefree and happy to nervous, anxious, and stressed out.

Just when I thought I'd moved past the challenges I faced in high school, they all started surfacing again, one by one. It began with the stomach troubles. This time, however, it was much worse. It was as if every move I made would impact my success in life; and as a result, I made myself sick before every exam and presentation, and even before my intramural basketball games. My body was not responding well to the pressure, and it began to rebel against me.

There were some big differences this time around that made everything more intense. The first was the fact that my belief that the harder I worked the more I would succeed was turning out to be completely false. I'd been putting in more effort than I ever had before, studying twice as long as anyone I knew. I was even the guy who people came to for answers the day before the exam because I was so prepared. The challenge was that most of my classes involved numbers. This was the year in business where I had to take all the core requirements, including finance, economics, and statistics. I was not a numbers person by nature, so these classes were extremely difficult for me. I studied for them using repetition and memory, and so whenever I had to answer a question that forced me to apply the learning to a new problem, I froze. On every exam I took, the professors found a way to put a couple of questions in that I had no idea how to answer. Every time this happened, I freaked out, had a minor panic attack, and ended up getting an unsatisfactory grade as a result. This fear even impacted my ability to do well on the questions that I *did* know how to answer. Not to mention, I was running to the bathroom five minutes before every test because my stomach was so upset.

The second challenge was that I now lived by myself. After spending the previous year surrounded by amazing people in my dorm, I wasn't able to find roommates, so I ended up getting my own apartment. When the stomach sickness came back, it kick-started a downward spiral, and my loneliness started to resurface. From there, the old feelings of depression popped up, because I'd placed my sense of value on being smart and doing well in school. If I couldn't even do that anymore, then where was my self-esteem going to come from? As the semester progressed, it seemed as if everything began to pile on top of me.

The next thing to come was physical injuries. During the previous summer, I'd started to experience pain in both of my feet. The physiotherapist called it *plantar fasciitis,* and simply put: the arches in my feet were inflamed. I was told that with a bit of treatment and arch supports, I wouldn't have any further issues. But with all the pressure of school, my feet kept getting worse instead of better. It got to a point where I could no longer stand for more than ten minutes without experiencing excruciating pain. As a result, I couldn't play nearly as many sports, and going out to parties and socializing became quite difficult.

My self-esteem continued to diminish, and the depression kept getting more intense. I had no outlet for my suffering, and there wasn't one area of my life where I truly felt happiness. The more I dwelled on all that was going wrong, the worse I felt, and the more often negative things would happen to me. I had no idea at this point that on some level I was in fact creating all of it, but

I was sure that this couldn't be what my life was supposed to be like. Everyone kept telling me to enjoy my time at college, because these were supposed to be the best years of my life. Ironically, this one felt like the worst.

॥ 回 卐

I remember the night that everything took a magical turn in a different direction. I had hit rock bottom as I was approaching the last month of the first semester. Allan was also studying at McGill, and whenever I was feeling really depressed and couldn't be alone, I'd called him to see if he wanted to have dinner. I went over to his apartment that night, and I told him everything I was going through. He wasn't equipped to help me with any of it, because he had his own challenges at the time, but he did suggest that I consider talking to our father. He said that Dad seemed to have made some big changes. I wasn't sure if he was just passing me off to someone else because he didn't want to take on my issues along with his own, or if he genuinely thought our father could help me.

Regardless, at this point I was willing to talk to anyone. My dad and I had had our fair share of differences, and an unspoken tension still existed between us. I hadn't really spoken to him in much depth over the past few years, yet something inside of me knew that I needed to give this a shot. I knew he'd gone through some major life changes recently, as Allan said, and I'd even started to see some of them when I went home to visit. Getting a little bit ahead of what he's shared so far in this book, I also knew that he'd decided to become a life coach, but I had no idea what that even was. I was desperate for any sort of help I could get, so I took Allan's advice.

The next day, I picked up the phone and, for the first time ever, I poured my heart out to my dad. I told him everything that I was going through—in detail. I'm not sure if he had any clue as to what I was experiencing up until that point, but by the end of the conversation he was well aware of it. He told me a little about what he wanted to do as a life coach and said he'd be happy to try and help me through this tough time. I wasn't ready to commit to anything, so he said to call him whenever I needed someone to talk to, and we could go from there. He also recommended that if I didn't feel comfortable speaking with him, I could try out the mental-health services at the university and speak to a psychiatrist.

I decided to go that route first, while still casually having conversations with my dad about all the stuff he'd learned. I also started to witness some big shifts in the way he was living his life and really started to believe that whatever he'd done had worked. I went to see the school psychiatrist for about four sessions, and it helped me process a lot of my childhood issues with my parents, primarily my father. This experience also made me feel more comfortable making a commitment to have my dad coach me on a regular basis. And so, I became one of his first students.

We started out speaking several times a week, since I was so vulnerable and desperate for support. Sometimes we even spoke many times a day. He began teaching me new philosophies, belief systems, and perspectives on life. From the first moment I heard all these amazing and inspiring ideologies, I knew on some level that I'd been waiting my whole life to be introduced to these teachings. As the saying goes, "When the student is ready, the teacher appears." At the beginning of 2005, I embarked on a new journey, and deep in my heart I knew that everything was finally beginning to turn around.

Chapter Five

TAKING A LEAP AND EMBRACING CHANGE

Jeffrey's Story

Although I still faced challenges, I had something I didn't have before—hope! I no longer felt desperate or out of control. I realized that I was in charge of my life, and by changing my thoughts and beliefs I could not only cope, but transform any issue into an opportunity for growth. Although I wasn't always sure how I was going to make the changes, I knew I could do it, and I came to realize that I was personally responsible for everything I was doing. A spark of excitement and energy began to form as I continued to get to know myself better and started to like the person I saw.

I was learning new techniques to shift my thoughts and create fresh perspectives on situations that didn't feel good. It required a lot of practice, but in constantly being aware of my thoughts and knowing that I had the power to change them, my old habits of fearful thinking began to slip away. I slowly started to feel more positive and as though I had more control over my circumstances. I realized that life was a journey, and as a result stopped pushing so hard to get to the finish line.

I maintained my meditation practice on a daily basis. This offered me moments of peace and tranquility in my hectic schedule. The more I learned to slow down my thoughts, the more I was able to keep them in check. I also continued to journal, and as I did so, my practice evolved. I started by pouring out my frustration, anger, and stresses onto the page, and then slowly found that through my free-flow writing I was beginning to receive advice from a power that was beyond my comprehension. It appeared that the practice of simply emptying my mind onto a piece of a paper was serving me well. I was able to allow this writing to come from a mindless place—perhaps my heart or spirit—and the messages that were surfacing were often quite profound. Later, I would come to understand that they were intuitive, and that I was finally learning to connect to my sixth sense.

Intuition

The definition that I feel best describes the term *intuition* is as follows: "the ability to acquire knowledge or a direct perception of truth or fact independent of any reasoning process or inference." In other words, it's an immediate understanding of a situation, topic, experience, or connection that comes naturally without any logic, reason, or analysis.

Intuition or Fear?

Since intuition can be as subtle as a sensation in the pit of your stomach or goose bumps on your arms, it's often hard to know if you're getting an intuitive nudge or if it's your mind once again telling you what to do. So what's the difference? What I've found is that intuition feels much lighter and fainter than the typical chatter in our heads that we face on a daily basis. An intuitive nudge is always kind and gentle, even when it's warning you of impending danger. It won't likely appear in a panicked way. Once you have started regularly tuning in to your intuition, you'll find that when you don't take heed of a message that's for your highest good, it will be repeated several times. Some say that when you get the same clear sign three times, it is definitely coming from your intuition.

This isn't to be confused with the obsessive mind that constantly repeats things over and over again, often in a disquieting fashion. The only way we've come to truly tell the difference between the two is in the way the message feels. Fear has a more urgent and terrifying pull, while intuition has more patience, reassurance, and certainty attached to it. Fear or mind chatter might sound something like this: *Oh my god, what if I'm really sick? I've had this backache for ages, what if it's something really bad? I could wind up in the hospital. I don't have time for that right now, I'm way too busy. What am I going to do?* Whereas an intuitive nudge might send you a strong, consistent hint to see your doctor about your backache. You'll likely find yourself saying: "I don't even know why I went to the doctor, but something inside me told me I really should get this checked out."

As intuition comes from the right side of the brain, it often seems happenstance rather than logical. Sometimes it's hard to explain altogether. Like our other senses (sight, sound, touch, smell, and taste) intuition doesn't speak to us in any given language. For these messages to be of benefit, they need to be interpreted or translated (this is what I was doing through my journaling). They're often not clear or concise, but rather just a knowing. Intuition always feels true despite the doubt that may surface alongside it. These qualms aren't coming from your intuition, but from your mind.

Since intuition is not logical, the left side of the brain often examines an intuitive sign in a critical way. This can cause internal conflict—should you listen to your gut or obey your brain? I believe that if you're able to overcome the judgment and start tuning in to your intuition on a regular basis, its messages will start to come across loud and clear, and you won't be able to ignore them, even if you try.

Now that I was on this journey, I began to meet all sorts of new people and learn things I'd never dreamed were possible. Because we were living in Ottawa, I had access to a wellness community that I previously didn't even realize existed. I discovered modalities that worked on the physical, mental, emotional, and spiritual aspects of my well-being. Because I wasn't putting in nearly as many hours in the business, I had more time to dedicate to these new methods. It was as though I were a student again, trying out all the different concepts and practices—but this time I was free to go at my own pace, pursuing what felt right for me.

I met regularly with a personal trainer and a massage therapist, had sessions with energy healers and an emotional intuitive, went for angel readings and shamanic healings, and worked with a holistic nutritionist. I went to Hay House conferences and empowerment workshops, listened to motivational speakers, and read every book in the self-help section of the bookstore. I even met one-on-one with a local rabbi in an attempt to find relevance and meaning in my own religion. I tried anything and everything that I thought would assist me on my journey. I created a sanctuary in the room that was formerly my office. I lit candles. I bought relaxation CDs. I listened to guided meditations. I decorated my space with inspiring quotes and photographs. I took on this experience with the same intensity that I'd applied to everything else in my life, but this time it felt so much more natural.

I'd become increasingly open-minded, and now I was willing to try anything. In the past I would have been disturbed by challenges to my existing way of thinking, but now I welcomed new perspectives, even if I didn't agree with them. I was pushing myself to get out of the linear thinking that had preoccupied me for so many years. The more comfortable I got with myself, the easier it was to accept new possibilities. The more open I was to this learning, the more opportunities showed up in my life.

To my surprise, I discovered that many people were on a similar journey. I found a community of people both in Ottawa and all over North America who were interested in the same things and searching for more meaning in their own lives. At the time, however, these individuals were predominantly women. And while I was fortunate enough to have my wife participating in most of these practices and workshops with me, it still required courage to be the only man in the room. Fortunately, this is no longer the case, and since then I've met and worked with many incredible men who are also embarking on similar paths.

With all of this change came a natural distancing from some relatives and friends whom I'd once been close with. I had never been one for small talk, and while I was eager to share my discoveries, not everyone wanted to hear about or accept what I was experiencing. I found myself at parties and social events surrounded by talk about all that was wrong with the world at a time when all I wanted to do was share my newfound positive outlook. Many individuals were turned off by or afraid to hear what I had to say. They'd dismiss it as "New Age" or "airy-fairy" or "not for them"— in hopes that I wouldn't shatter their seemingly secure and traditional views. As a result, I avoided certain situations or sat quietly when I felt my insights would be unwelcome.

But it wasn't all social isolation. What I gained was a vibrant network of like-minded individuals who were eager to learn more and wanted to share in my discoveries. I found people with more knowledge than I had, those whom I was able to learn from, and those who were eager to learn from me. I recognized my passion for learning and teaching, and realized that sharing with and helping others was something I had to do more of as I continued to transform my life.

🖾 🔲 🖾

My next coach came to me, not unlike the first, in a rather serendipitous way. Prior to coming to work for us, one of the senior managers at our company had taken a course in Toronto with a woman by the name of Elfreda Pretorius. He suggested we all have dinner together the next time we were in Toronto. Elfreda was a life coach, author, and speaker whose work focused on mind-body healing and personal growth.

From that dinner I found myself with a new life coach, and suddenly I was digging deep into my personal history to figure out who I really was. With her assistance, I was able to reflect on and review my past from a more objective point of view. I uncovered belief systems that were so entrenched in my unconscious mind that I didn't even know they existed. Through emotional coaching sessions, extensive journaling, and soul searching, I was able to shift the beliefs that no longer served me and begin building new ones. Elfreda opened my eyes to yet another aspect of my personal journey: spirituality. She helped create the space for me to look within and discover a newfound faith in a great power that I hadn't had before. All of this gave me a greater sense of comfort and calm, and a knowing that there was more to life than what I was experiencing in the physical world.

Opportunities for learning continued to present themselves as I went through some very challenging times at work. My plan to have the company run by professional managers was not working out as well as I had hoped, and I came to realize that I wasn't a very firm leader. I cared more about people than profits, so while I'd set goals and expectations for my employees, I had trouble holding them accountable when targets weren't met. In the business world, this does not bode well for financial success.

Since I wasn't achieving great results and no longer felt comfortable in my leadership role, I wanted to have less to do with the company. However, I felt guilty giving up the family business that I'd worked so hard to build. And besides, what would I do all day if I didn't go to the office? My old beliefs were playing on a loop inside my head: *How can I sit at home while others are hard at work? If I'm not going to be a contributing member of the workforce, where will my worth come from? I'm only in my early 50s; that's way too young to retire.* I knew I didn't enjoy the job as much as I once had, but what else would I do?

Around this time, our company began to face financial challenges, and the manager we'd hired expressed a desire to take on more responsibility. Since I wanted to be less involved and he wanted to be more involved, I surrendered my day-to-day duties and passed the reins to him. Now all I had to do was find something to occupy my time.

That's when the idea of becoming a life coach first dawned on me. I was passionate about what I was learning and had a deep desire to share with others. Unlike in my previous life, I didn't approach my new career direction with a formal business plan. Instead, there seemed to be a higher power that nudged me to move away from corporate life and into the world of coaching. I started to spread the word that I was doing this type of work, and slowly clients began to filter in. My first referral for a paying client came from my sister, and in working with him I began to develop my coaching style. The more time I spent working with people, the more I was sure that this was my calling.

Now this was also around the same time that Michael was going through some fairly serious challenges at university. I saw this as a great opportunity to use some of the skills I'd recently acquired to help one of my children. As Michael and I began chatting more and more by phone, and as I started sharing what I'd been learning on my journey, I noticed a bond forming that I'd never before shared with my son. We were developing a mutual sense of respect—I was no longer the authoritative father figure, but a coach and a guide to a young person struggling with the same issues I'd faced in my life. This was a great turning point in our relationship. I no longer wanted to control Michael and tell him what to do; rather, I was eager to share with him what I'd been taught so he, too, could benefit from this wisdom.

It was through working with both Michael and the manager who'd taken over the running of our company that I learned a great deal about empowerment. A common definition for *empower* is: "to give power or authority to, or to enable or permit." I realized that growing up I never really felt empowered. From a young age, it seemed to me that most people were eager to take away my power. I came to realize that I had been disempowered by my parents, siblings, teachers, and friends, because I listened to what everyone else had to say and always did what I was told.

No matter what I accomplished, I always tended to feel as if I weren't good enough. Only once I understood this did I realize that I'd been doing the same thing to the people who mattered most to me. I began to question my parenting and leadership style: *Is it possible that by telling Michael what to do and how to do it, I depleted his sense of self-confidence? Did I disempower him as a child, causing him to resent me as a parent? Am I controlling the people I work with in the office, rather than encouraging them to figure things out for themselves?*

What I discovered is that when you treat others with respect and trust their ability to succeed, they often rise to a level of competence that far exceeds your expectations. When you empower them, it's as if you light a spark within them that says, "I know you have what it takes to do this!" And lo and behold, they often do. If, on the other hand, you control people by telling them what to do, you're sending them a message that they're incapable of figuring things out on their own.

Although we often do this from a place of not wanting the person to fail or get in trouble, and although our motives are usually not deceitful, nonetheless we're disempowering or taking power away. When we empower someone, we are really saying, "I have faith in you and know you can do it." We inspire them to find the strength within.

While working with Michael and the manager in our company, I learned that empowering them not only made them feel good about themselves, but made me feel good about myself, too. It was a win-win. Putting the power into their hands was so incredible that I knew it would be incorporated into my mission as a life coach. I'd set out to empower as many people as I could.

What came next was the understanding that if I wasn't fortunate enough to have others empower me, I'd have to do it for myself. If I didn't have someone who truly believed in me, then I'd have to truly believe in myself. I was beginning to witness how the process of empowering others seemed to unlock hidden talents within them, and I wanted that for myself, too. I became fascinated with the subject of self-worth and personal responsibility and began to reflect on how I'd lost so much inner confidence over the years.

Personal Responsibility: What I Know Now

I've come to believe that in order to take personal responsibility for your life, you must genuinely love and respect yourself. If you've spent most of your time thinking that you're not good enough, you'll most likely have trouble taking ownership for everything that happens to you today.

To help reclaim personal responsibility, it's important to get to know yourself *without* judgment. Try looking at yourself as if for the first time, and focus on all your best qualities. The more you're able to like what you see, the more willing you will be to take ownership for all of your thoughts, words, and actions. If you're going to accomplish your goals and dreams, you must trust in your ability to do so successfully, and you must believe that you are worthy of these accomplishments.

Overcoming fear is another key to taking personal responsibility. When this emotion dictates your direction in life and influences your choices, you'll tend to find yourself making excuses and blaming others. By doing so, you're giving away your power, not embracing it. If you genuinely believe that there's an external force preventing you from doing what you want, or that it's someone else's fault that you're not successful, then you're openly accepting the fact that what you want is *not* within your control. If you believe that other people or circumstances have more power than you do, then you're basically sentencing yourself to a life of being limited by others. If, on the other hand, you choose to overcome your fears and realize how much power you truly have, then you can, through personal responsibility, begin to create the life you desire.

Some of the fear-based excuses that I came up against included: *I'm not smart enough, I don't have enough money, my family doesn't support me,* and *I'm not worthy of success.* These, or variations of them, are common to most people. Excuses tend to leave you feeling helpless and prevent you from coming up with a solution to the problem you're addressing. When I finally learned how to shift from my fears to statements such as: *I am smart enough, I have all that I need, I am capable of supporting myself,* and *I am worthy,* I instantly felt more empowered.

It's easy to get caught up in a cycle of excuses and always find someone or something else to blame. The more of them you make, the more you start to believe that they're your truth. This is extremely disempowering. You simply convince yourself that you can't do anything meaningful about any situation—and so you just let life happen *to* you. With every excuse that you make, you give your power away to some other person or circumstance. This behavior typically leads to blaming. An excuse places fault with someone else. And while it does let you off the hook, it leaves you with no choice but to sit back and passively watch as your life unfolds. When something doesn't go your way, you become defensive and blame others or "life" for your misfortunes.

I was stuck in this blame cycle for many years before I woke up and realized that I wasn't dealing with the actual issues I faced, but rather directing my emotions and frustrations onto someone else. I'll give you an example. When Michael, or any of my kids for that matter, didn't do well on a test or an assignment, their default response would often be to start blaming the teacher. Their first reactions would be to say things like: "It wasn't fair," "The test was way too hard," "I hate this teacher," "He didn't prepare me at all," "I can't believe he marked my paper that way," or "I doubt he even read it." In responding this way, they'd put all their energy into blame instead of focusing on how they could turn this low grade around.

The first step in taking personal responsibility for a situation like this is to ask yourself, "What can I learn from this, and how can I do better next time?" From a personally responsible perspective, you may come up with ideas such as: I can study more for the next exam, I can go to the teacher for extra help, I can pay better attention in class, I can ask the teacher for her suggestions on how to boost my grade, I can find a tutor to help me better understand the subject matter, and so on. No matter what the circumstances are, if you take personal responsibility, you'll always come up with possible solutions that can improve your situation, whereas if you blame others or yourself, you'll remain stuck in a place of negativity where no change is possible.

御 回 司

As my work as a coach increased, I started to find patterns and trends in the issues many people were facing. It was fascinating to me when I realized that no matter what individuals were doing, how they outwardly presented themselves, how much they accomplished, or how high their socioeconomic status was, deep down most of them were struggling with an inability to love themselves.

The more intimately I became acquainted with the inner feelings and thoughts of those I was working with, the more I discovered this commonality. The basis of most clients' struggles was the same: a lack of self-esteem and self-worth. What I know now is that this lack of self-love has become an epidemic that most people in our society struggle with in some way or another. Whether you realize it or not, the ability to love yourself is extremely powerful. It didn't take me long to figure out that if I was going to be able to help others learn to love themselves, I'd have to do some work on myself first. (Have you ever tried looking at yourself in the mirror and saying, "I love you"? If just the thought of doing so makes you uncomfortable, then this is the perfect place to begin.)

As I continued to learn about myself and develop increased inner confidence, I found that I was able to be more at ease with who I truly was. I was not only becoming comfortable with my strengths, but with my weaknesses as well. I realized that I didn't have to be perfect in everything—as a matter of fact, I didn't really have to be perfect at *anything*. I just had to try my best. And if I loved myself enough, then I could stop trying to prove my worth to others. Once I learned to accept myself the way I was, the opinions of others no longer mattered.

But like everything, this was a work in progress. It's easy to love yourself unconditionally one day and feel totally desolate and self-critical the next. The journey to complete self-acceptance is a long one, and I'm still on it today. I've learned to be gentle with myself and forgiving of the times when, for whatever reason, my self-worth plummets. I've come to acknowledge all of who I am, including the parts I don't like.

I've also come to understand that the more I'm feeling empowered and the more the people around me are, too, the better I get along with them and the more respect, compassion, understanding, and love there is in our relationships. So whether you're fortunate enough to have someone who's empowering you in your life, or whether you choose to do so yourself, I encourage you to take back your power and realize that you're not only good enough, you're great!

Can you imagine how much better our world would be if we all felt confident enough about ourselves and had a deep sense of self-worth?

Retraining your mind to believe things about yourself when your experiences have reinforced the opposite can be a slow process. One of the techniques that Elfreda taught me turned out to be incredibly effective, although it required a real commitment. First, she had me write ten statements about what I wanted to create in my life. Although this may sound quite simple, the process of coming up with the ten most important things was quite challenging. My initial attempt produced a list of over 30 things, so I needed to distill it down. This exercise in and of itself was extremely revealing, as it forced me to truly reflect on those aspects that were the most critical. Then I had to turn my list into affirmations, using the correct wording to help invoke the Law of Attraction. I learned that I had to be concise, ensure I phrased what I wanted as if I already had it, and make sure the sentence was in the present tense. Here's the list I came up with at the time:

1. I am confident, and I am my own person.

2. I am courageous, and I overcome all my fears.

3. I am objective, and I always see the big picture.

4. I am always positive, and challenges are my opportunities.

5. Everything in my life is always in balance.

6. I believe in abundance.

7. I seek first to understand others and always see the good in people and events.

8. I am always in the flow.

9. I am guided by Source, and everything works for my higher good.

10. I unconditionally love myself.

Once I finalized my list, what came next was very interesting. Elfreda instructed me to write out each affirmation five times in the morning and five times in the evening for an entire month. So twice each day for a month, I diligently sat at my desk with my journal in quiet reflection and put to paper my affirmations. I was open to this process, but didn't really think much about whether it would work or not. I can't honestly tell you that as soon as I finished my 30 days of writing out these sentences, things magically changed. However, what I can say is that over the years I've unequivocally come to adopt these affirmations as my beliefs; and as a result, my behaviors have changed for the better. So, too, has my life.

回 回 回

While I continued my progress through reading, coaching, and practicing, what changed me the most wasn't something that happened within my mind, but within my heart. Through this experience, I was able to discover a part of me that had been buried for a long time—my feelings. I learned that the consciousness of the mind and that of the heart are two very different things. What most of us seek are happiness, peace, contentment, joy, satisfaction, pleasure, appreciation, recognition, respect, and, most of all, love. These are all feelings, yet we try tirelessly to attain them by using our minds. Feelings, by their very nature, are of the moment, the ultimate *now*. Our minds, on the other hand, can be all over the place, from past to present to future within the span of a second. As I realized all this, I wondered, *How am I ever going to get the things I so desperately want in my life if I am unable to feel? How can I achieve happiness if all I am capable of doing is thinking and not feeling deeply?*

Shutting down my feelings at a young age had adversely impacted not only my emotional well-being but also my physical body. I knew my maladies were centered in my gastrointestinal area, but I didn't realize that this, too, was the place of my emotional issues. I'll never forget my first experience with a shamanic healer who told me that all of my unexpressed emotions had crystallized in my gut. As he worked on this area of my body, I suddenly burst into tears, moving into the fetal position and coughing uncontrollably as I started to release the pent-up emotions that had lain dormant for so many years. While this experience was a bit shocking, I felt so much better after it was complete. It turned out that this was the first of many such treatments by different practitioners that eventually helped me to let go of the unprocessed emotions I'd been storing in my gut. This was only the beginning of my journey to get in touch with the "feeling" part of me.

Once I cleared away the multitude of unexpressed emotions, I found myself able to truly feel again. This turned out to be one of the greatest indicators that things were changing for the better. Growing up, I'd been taught that feelings were for girls and the only way to get ahead in the world was to be a good thinker. Therefore, I'd spent a lot of time developing my intellectual capacity, and now I was discovering a part of me that had been inactive for way too long. It was about to change my life dramatically—I could feel! And I was learning to express my feelings more freely. For the first time, I cried when I was sad. I cried when I was happy. I cried during movies. I allowed myself to be afraid. I gave myself permission to be tired. I let myself experience guilt and shame, to feel joy and, most important, love. The ability to feel opened up a whole new dimension in my world. In order to continue, I needed to work on not judging my emotions when they came up. Instead of lambasting myself for crying, I accepted the tears and let them flow through me.

What I realized is that so many people think that these lower and slower emotions (fear, anger, sadness, shame, guilt, exhaustion, and so on) are bad and should be repressed, while the higher and faster emotions (happiness, joy, love, peace, pride, contentment, and excitement) are good and should be embraced. But when we stop judging emotions altogether, it's so much easier to allow them to move through us in a healthy way—which, I believe, is what they're meant to do.

Yin and Yang:
the Delicate Balance of Head and Heart

According to Asian philosophy, emotions are a major part of what makes up our *yin,* or feminine, energy, while logic makes up our *yang,* or masculine, side. These two contrasting energies are present within each of us, and our challenge is to find the balance that allows us to feel comfortable with both. Although some associate yin with women and yang with men, I don't believe this is accurate. The traditional characteristics of yin include creativity, flexibility, and gentleness (the feeling and being), whereas the traits of yang include focus, activity, alertness, and planning (the doing). While these are respectively associated with the feminine and masculine, they don't just pertain to men and women. Most males have some feminine energy and most women have masculine energy. The key is to find the harmony of having both, and that can be challenging, especially if you subscribe to a more traditional belief that men must be masculine and women must be feminine. This stereotyping has caused many problems and challenges as people struggle to be someone or something they're not.

There was a time in history when the yin energy was far more respected and honored. Unfortunately, we've moved to a moment in human evolution where more of the world seems to value yang energy. It's the doing, thinking, pushing, competing, and accomplishing that seems to be rewarded. Society doesn't encourage sensitivity and creativity; rather, these characteristics tend to be minimized and often frowned upon.

Sadly, many yin-leaning individuals have been made to feel inadequate or valued less as a result. This is increasingly difficult for "feelers," because they experience this sense of inadequacy or not fitting in more intensely than those who are more naturally yang in their makeup. You might think, then, that yang-leaning people have an easier time in life, but this is likely not the case either, because they have forsaken an essential part of themselves—their feelings. The balance, whether for you it's 20 percent yang to 80 percent yin or 40 percent yin and 60 percent yang, is essential if you want to live a contented life.

There have been significant societal shifts over the past few decades that have led both women and men to abandon their yin in order to succeed in the workplace and survive in an increasingly expensive and consumption-based world. People go to work to pay for the things they believe they need in order to feel worthy. They enroll their kids in activities —specifically, competitive sports and enriching academic programs—so they'll be considered well-rounded. Parents push their children to do well in school so that they'll be viewed as smart and successful. And then they heap loads of pressure upon themselves to spend time with their kids, exercise, keep the house clean, and make enough money, all in the name of balance. But none of this is yin energy.

Most of us ignore our compassionate and creative sides that are so eager to get out. That inner feminine energy is begging us to slow down and enjoy life. We push and push and push, and we get run down, depressed, and sick as a result . . . and then we wonder why.

Thankfully, there is a shift taking place as people move toward living a more yin-centered life. Yoga studios are popping up all over the place, play-centered learning is becoming popular again among educators of young children, and people are being encouraged to take more time for themselves. In order to live a truly balanced and happy life, we must embrace all parts of ourselves. That means we have to experience and express our emotions, enjoy slowness, play with our kids, embrace imperfection, accept our children no matter how well they do in sports and academics, take on creative projects, practice doing nothing, and enjoy life. Sometimes we'll feel sad, and when we do, we must let ourselves cry. Sometimes we'll feel happy, and in those moments we must let ourselves laugh out loud.

When Michael was a child, he was extremely sensitive—but because I was coming from such a yang-centered place, I didn't know how to nurture or understand this behavior. He had trouble understanding his own feelings and, as he's mentioned, experienced great discomfort when it came to trying to fit in. He also loved sports and was very competitive. This was his yang side, and it was much more accepted by his peers. As Michael repressed his sensitivity and emotional side, his competitive side became more aggressive and angry. He wasn't living in balance. It is critical to understand that we all have both yin and yang energies present within us. No one can possess just one without the other, so finding our own balance and helping young people find theirs is essential for a more content and well-adjusted population.

With my newfound ability to balance yin and yang—thinking and feeling—my life seemed so much fuller and less stressful. What I hadn't realized was that by getting in touch with my yin, I would be able to tune in to the internal guidance system (intuition) required to reconstruct and build a new set of beliefs that would serve me well. I was about to embark on the stage of my journey where I would develop and firm up the philosophies that would guide me forward toward a brighter future. It was an incredibly empowering time in my life.

Michael's Story

I was 19 years old and ready to create positive change in my life. I'd endured so many challenges full of pain and suffering, and my breaking point was when it became clear that things could not go on as they were. I am so grateful that the Universe heard my cry for help and sent me a fantastic resource—my father. If he had not made the changes in his life first, mine as I know it today would be completely different.

I remember that when I was in high school, my dad used to say to me, "Michael, a relationship is a two-way street. If you want to have a relationship with me, you have to meet me halfway." At the time, however, I didn't feel as though he was coming halfway to meet me, nor did we ever discuss what halfway would look like for each of us. As a result, we disconnected from one another and didn't have much of a relationship. Now things were much different.

As he described, my father had made some big changes: he'd spent a lot of time clearing his own issues from the past and was ready to share his experiences with me. He took the first step with the empowered action in his own life; then he came more than halfway and extended his hand to support me. He spoke to me with such kindness and love that it was as if I was talking to an entirely different person. His rigidness and controlling nature had disappeared. What was left was this sensitive, compassionate, patient, understanding, and incredibly supportive man who I really didn't know very well.

A big part of what allowed me to open up so quickly and easily to him was that I felt as though I were speaking to someone who didn't even resemble the father I'd known growing up. Sure, subtle tendencies from the past would surface throughout our coaching, but for the most part I was talking to a person who'd taken the necessary steps to improve his own life, and this inspired me to do the same. If he could do it at 51, then I could certainly do it at 19. So we began this new journey of father and son, coach and student, mentor and mentee, and built the foundation for what would flourish into a wonderful friendship years down the road.

There were a few simple yet profound principles that I learned right off the bat, and these allowed me to start shifting my perception of life, opening my mind to new ways of thinking, and easing the suffering I'd been experiencing. The first lesson I learned came from one of Robin Sharma's quotes: "Awareness precedes choice and choice precedes change." I realized that if I wanted to make a change to the circumstances that were creating all the pain and suffering, then I had to make the choice to do something different. However, before I was able to make more empowered decisions, I needed to become more aware of what enabled me to make those choices.

During my entire life I'd felt powerless, believing that I'd simply been sent experiences, with no choice but to accept them or feel miserable. What I learned is that I not only had the ability to change the situations and feelings I once thought were permanent, but also that I was actually responsible for creating them in the first place. This was an extremely empowering concept for me to grasp, because for the first time it was as if there were something I could do to change the outcome of my life.

Everything that was going on within me was directly contributing to what was happening outside of me. After taking in this principle, I wanted to jump right ahead to the "change" part. If I was creating all the challenges, pain, and suffering, then I wanted to snap my fingers and make it all stop—now! Well, my dad was there to remind me that this process takes time. The outcomes we've created are all based on habits, actions, words, and thoughts that we have been living (unconsciously) for most of our lives. Therefore, reshaping all of these into different outcomes requires time, practice, and patience. This was not easy for me to accept, because I didn't want to be patient; after all, I never had been and just wanted to make all of it go away immediately.

To help ease my frustration, my dad had me focus on one thing at a time. He said, "If you want things to change, you have to make empowered choices. But before you can start doing that, you need to focus more on your awareness. Without awareness, there is no empowerment. And without empowerment, I wouldn't have been able to make choices that felt better; and thus, I wouldn't have been able to create positive change in my life."

What came next was the realization that all of my life experiences were, in fact, influenced by how I was thinking. Did you know that the average person has approximately 50,000 to 80,000 thoughts each day? I had no idea. When you stop to think about this number, you realize how much is actually going on inside our minds at all times. If, in fact, we're not really aware of these thoughts—which was certainly the case for me—then is it possible that we're not really aware of the reality we're creating for ourselves? When I realized this, it was a huge breakthrough for me. If I had the power to control my thoughts, and if my thoughts had the power to influence my life, then all I had to do was choose better thoughts. Well, this was easier said than done.

In order to get control of all those things running through my head, the first step was to simply become aware of them. What were they all anyway, and where were they coming from? Awareness makes you feel empowered, and when you're empowered you're able to make better choices. Dad taught me that in order to be aware of my thoughts, I first had to slow them down so that I could actually listen to them. A helpful practice for this was the action of keeping a daily-thoughts journal—a place where I could write down everything going on inside my head. (To learn how to create a *Daily-Thoughts Journal,* see the Resources section.) When you put your thoughts into writing, you can see them more clearly. A great way to understand this is to think about the garbage in your home. You know that you have to take the trash out regularly, or your living space begins to stink. The same is true for our minds. If we don't dump out the "trash thoughts" every so often, our minds get cluttered, disorganized, and stinky.

Another practice to help slow down the mind is meditation. If you've ever watched Formula One racing, you'll notice that when a car experiences mechanical problems, the driver slows down and goes into the pit for the necessary repairs, since they can't be made when the car is going 160 miles per hour. It would only make sense that in order to "service" your thoughts you must first slow them down.

I found meditation to be an amazing practice, but it took me a while to learn how to do it effectively. Basically, when you sit quietly and listen to what's going on in your head, you're better equipped to let go of the thoughts that aren't serving you and replace them with more positive, empowering ones. You can't do this when you're trying to do a million other things—or driving your race car. I created a space in my apartment where I could sit in a comfortable chair and listen to a guided meditation CD (see *Meditation* in the Resources section for a link to purchase Jeffrey's meditation audio program). This really helped me learn how to meditate. In the beginning, I'd turn to this practice only as a way to help calm my nerves when I felt really stressed, but as I did it more frequently and realized the amazing benefits, I started to make it a part of my daily routine. It was amazing how much calmer I started to feel.

Once I'd learned how to slow down my thoughts, I began to take inventory of them, and realize that most had been based on fear and negativity. My dad walked me through various ways I could start changing them. This process began by identifying all of the negative, fear-based thoughts that I had on a regular basis. Some examples are: *I am not good enough, I am going to fail and my life will be over, Life is too hard,* and *I can't handle this.* The list went on. I realized that almost everything going through my head was not only negative but was beating me down rather than building me up. I had become my biggest critic instead of my biggest fan.

My dad explained that I could substitute destructive thoughts, feelings, and actions with ones that felt better—but the key to knowing whether they needed changing was what he called a *feel check.* To perform this test, first bring your awareness to whatever is in your mind, and then consider: *How does this make me feel?*

Getting in touch with my feelings wasn't super hard for me, because I was naturally quite sensitive. So once I determined that a thought didn't feel very good, I had to make the choice to substitute something that felt better. Instead of *I am not good enough,* I tried out *I love myself exactly how I am.* Instead of *I am going to fail,* I tried *I am going to learn the material to the best of my ability and release my attachment to the outcome. Life is too hard* became *Life is a wonderful journey of learning and growth.* And instead of *Why me?* I thought, *Yes, me, bring it on!*

While this seems relatively straightforward, some of these things that I'd been telling myself were much harder to shift than others. For example, I'd spent the past dozen or so years believing that life was a race; I had to get good grades to be successful; and if I didn't get a degree and a good job, I was worthless. These beliefs were so ingrained in my subconscious that they were quite difficult to transform. Before I could simply replace these fear-based thoughts with faith-based ones, I had to alter my perception of the situation surrounding them. A quote that really helped me with this process came from Hay House author Dr. Wayne W. Dyer. He said: "When you change the way you look at things, the things you look at change."

I had to start changing the way I looked at my life, my education, and my future. Once I was able to see everything from a different vantage point (I'll get to what this actually was later in the chapter), I was able to start thinking more positively and in ways that supported me—and actually believing in what I was doing.

As I started to shift my thoughts, the words that I spoke to others began to shift, too, as did my actions. This process took a lot of practice and patience, but every positive experience helped to reshape the negative ones stored in my subconscious. One step at a time, everything began to change. I remember the winter day in 2005 when I first felt what my dad referred to as my *higher self.* I was walking home from class as it was snowing, and I felt this huge rush of joy move through my entire body. I decided to play in the snow the way I had as a kid, slipping and sliding on the ice and skipping while humming a happy tune. For the first time, I wasn't worried about what others would think of me; I was so content that nothing else mattered. Life certainly was beginning to change for the better.

᯼ ◎ ᯼

As I've stated, I was taught at a young age, ironically by my father, that life is a race and the first one to the finish line wins. The person who has the most thoughts, the most accomplishments, and the most money is the winner when all is said and done.

In coaching with my dad, he and I began to reprogram this belief. It turns out this had been contributing to much of my suffering. My dad replaced the old lesson with something much more empowering and less fear based. He explained, "Life is more about the journey and less about the destination. There is no need to rush, because everything will unfold when it's supposed to." My focus shifted to learning from every step, every experience along the way, rather than jumping from one destination to the next. I used to live based on the events in my calendar. I'd focus on the next exam, the next sporting event, the next party—planning and stressing in preparation for whatever was coming up next. I always used to say, "When this exam is over, I'll be happy again," or "If we win the basketball game, I'll feel better about myself." But instead of being happy or feeling better, I'd finish one ordeal feeling uneasy and immediately turn my focus to the next thing.

By focusing on the journey instead of the destination, it no longer really mattered where I was heading; more important was what I was learning along the way. Life became much simpler, and the pressure I felt began to lift. *What if the purpose of life is learning, growing, and evolving as a person?* I began to think. Everything else would essentially stem from that. My perception completely changed once I started applying this concept to all aspects of my life. School was different, because I was no longer focused on the grades or what they were going to get me. I was now concentrated on learning. Every event that used to be such a big deal became a great opportunity to grow. I studied for understanding instead of simply for good grades. As a result, the pressure began to dissolve, and so did my stomach pains. After six months of really applying this belief, my stomach problems completely disappeared. And, to my amazement, my grades began to improve significantly. All it took was a shift in perspective.

The same thing happened for sports and social events. I was no longer a nervous wreck before an intramural game or before going out to a party. I started removing the significance from each of these events or destination points and seeing them as equal opportunities to learn and grow—as small steps on my journey. I'd constantly have to remind myself to slow down and not race through the process, and eventually I began to have faith that all would work out for the best, and for *my* best. My desire to control everything outside of myself began to disintegrate as my trust in life grew stronger. I embraced the natural flow of events, taking things one step at a time and watching the magic unfold in front of me. I actually started to feel happiness—true, genuine happiness. My depression was a thing of the past, and things were becoming simple again.

The next concept I learned was based around beliefs. My dad always said that the human brain only does what we've taught it to do. Therefore, our thinking, perspectives, and views are all a result of our conditioning. I'd constantly recite old beliefs to my dad, based on something I'd been taught as a young boy, and he'd question whether this was true in my heart or something I'd been taught to perceive as real. At first I resisted this process, because many of these beliefs were not only deeply rooted from my childhood, but had come from the very man who was now prompting me to question their validity. My dad would say, "Question all of your beliefs. Your heart will know what is real for you." This remains one of the most instrumental lessons I've learned on my journey, and it continues to allow me to grow and evolve today.

With coaching from my father, I began to question and reshape my beliefs to feel better. The purpose of school became learning more about myself and the subject I was studying. My success in the classroom no longer determined my value—my heart did. I no longer relied on others' judgments, and instead placed value on how I saw myself through my own eyes. One by one, I questioned and then shifted all of the limiting and self-destructive beliefs that had been causing my pain and suffering for years and holding me back from experiencing my true potential. As my beliefs began to take on a new, better-feeling form, I began to experience true freedom, infinite potential and opportunity, and joy in its purest state. This was the beginning step in discovering, and then living, my authentic self, and I felt better than ever.

The best part about this new journey was how quickly my relationship began to transform with my dad. For my first 18 years we were rivals, never saw eye to eye, and never truly listened to one another. Now it was as if our relationship had made a 180-degree turn. We were communicating clearly and compassionately with one another and working together. I finally was able to feel genuine love and support from my father. I'd been longing for this for so many years, and although in the early stages I still harbored resentment that I hadn't had this love and attention when I was a child, my resentment quickly dissolved when I decided to embrace what was happening in the present moment.

When my dad and I used to talk, we'd both get stuck in our own opinions and perspectives, and neither of us would allow the other to be right. Both of us wanted to come out on top, so simple conversations would turn to nasty arguments very quickly. But now as I followed my father's lead, my desire to be right began to transform into the desire to be free. He would ask me, "Michael, do you want to be right or do you want to be free?" My heart always answered, "Free," and that was my reminder that I was likely trying to control something or prove my value by getting validation.

Whenever we faced resistance in our discussions, he wouldn't give up and walk away or hang up the phone like he used to. He stuck with it, trying to present his message in a way that would resonate with me. Sometimes I ended a call with my dad still feeling that resistance; however, I discovered very quickly that self-reflection would allow me to grow and apply what I'd just received. I often called him back a few hours later and said, "I get it now, and I apologize for fighting." He'd always accept my apology with compassion and show even more love. There was no desire in him to say, "I told you so," because he'd worked on being free instead of being right long before teaching this concept to me. Coaching me was his way of practicing all of what he'd learned and further integrating it into his own life.

How to Transform Your Relationships:
Seek First to Understand

What shifted in my relationship with my dad was his ability to change the way he looked at me and my perspective when we began our coaching sessions. Through his own work, he'd come to believe that in order to truly understand people, you must look at things from their point of view—seeking to understand where they're coming from rather than imposing your own ideas on them.

There are many factors that play important roles in this process. Observing a person's external environment, lifestyle choices, cultural background, family life, and childhood allows us to get a better appreciation of why he or she sees life in a specific way. This broadens our scope, helps us look beyond our own vantage point, and allows us to see life through someone else's lens. When we look at an individual from our own perspective, we are seeing him or her through our own conditioning, experiences, and judgments. However, if we truly want to put ourselves in another's shoes, we need to understand what he or she has been through and been taught to believe. This understanding is the foundation for creating a healthy relationship with your spouse, children, co-workers—even your boss or teacher.

While it's impossible to see life completely from other people's perspectives (because only in the movies can a person transform into someone else), at least if you can obtain a better understanding of where they're coming from you'll be more equipped to respond with compassion, empathy, and kindness. When we allow ourselves to understand other viewpoints, our reactions, decisions, and experiences involving them change.

There was a time while my dad was still running his business that a great deal of conflict emerged between various departments, resulting in poor customer service and inefficient operational practices. He explained to me that managers were frustrated their team members weren't cooperating with members of other departments throughout the company.

One of the employees came up with a solution to this conflict in the form of a program that was intended to promote more understanding and cooperation amongst the different areas. The program was called, "Walk a Mile in My Shoes." It required each employee to take a turn shadowing someone from a different department with whom they interacted in an operational function. This turned out to be a great success, because it gave all employees the opportunity to really see what their co-workers did on a daily basis. They also gained insight into how interconnected all of their duties were. Seeing each task from another person's perspective ultimately created greater cooperation, enabling the job to get done in a more effective and efficient manner. Everyone was a winner, including the customers, employees, and the company.

Because my dad was able to walk a mile in my shoes, he came at our coaching practice in a different way than he'd approached our father-son relationship up until that point. He was finally able to see that while I wasn't exactly like him— and was never going to be—I could still absorb and implement the same practices he'd benefited from, just in my own way. With this in mind, he was able to help me by using methods that worked best for me personally. I not only learned how to change my life, but also how to see my dad and other important people in my life from a place of more understanding.

The best part of being coached by my dad was that he never did anything *for* me, but always empowered me to do it on my own. He was there for guidance, support, and unconditional love, but would never go to battle for me. Prior to our working together, he was always trying to tell me how to do things. Now he was simply sharing his perspective and experience and encouraging me to discover my own truths. "Do what makes your heart content, Michael. I don't have all the answers for you. You have them within yourself," was his advice.

Through my growing and evolving relationship with my dad, I began to feel more confident and slowly became more comfortable with making my own decisions. The more I learned to trust my inner voice, the easier it all became. My dad made the whole process easier for me. He supported me no matter what. If I fell, he let me fall but was there with love and support to ease the pain I'd brought upon myself. He'd then empower me to learn from the experience and move forward. By the end of that year, I was a completely different person. With his support, I'd turned my breakdown into a breakthrough.

Chapter Six

INSPIRED LIVING, EMPOWERED ACTION

Michael's Story

My third and fourth years of university were an entirely different experience than my first two years. I'd been on my journey for eight months when I started my third year, and I was well on my way to reshaping the way that I thought, spoke, and acted. I was shedding old beliefs and paradigms that I'd been taught by my parents, my teachers, and the rest of society, and replacing them with new ones that I chose for myself. I was coaching with my dad weekly, sometimes more often, and applying all that I was learning every day at school.

Life was truly becoming one big learning experience, and my focus was on growing as an individual, not on getting good grades. Each moment was another opportunity to rewrite my story with a positive outlook. As I did, my experiences began to transform tremendously. Attending classes became much more enjoyable, as

I was actually interested in gaining more knowledge on the subjects rather than decoding the secret to success. Even the subjects that I'd previously found boring were tolerable now, because I'd developed a way of shifting my perspective to focus on absorbing something new.

The changes I'd made were not just apparent to me and my dad; my friends were noticing as well. I remember in my last year of school walking through the library during exam time. This was typically a very depressing time of year for students, as they struggled to cram way too much information into their brains in hopes of achieving good marks. Most of them were walking around with their heads down and making themselves sick with worry and stress. I, on the other hand, was very content, had a big smile on my face, and was embracing this wonderful experience and learning from it moment by moment.

My friends would come up to me somewhat shocked and ask what I was on and if I had any more of it for them. I told them it was self-love and positive, supportive thinking, and that I was happy to show them how to practice both. I began to share all that I'd been taught the previous couple of years with whoever was willing to listen. It was a great way for me to further integrate the learning into my life. There were only a few friends interested in what I had to share, but the process was so incredibly empowering for me. I knew then that helping others was what I was here on this planet to do.

When I graduated from university, it was thrilling to see how far I'd come. I'd spent the better part of the last two and a half years really working on bettering myself and my life, and I was experiencing the results on a daily basis. I was offered a corporate job in Toronto before I even graduated, and although I knew deep in my heart that it wasn't what I was supposed to be doing for the rest of my life, it felt like what I was supposed to do at that point. I knew that if I could make such a huge transition and shift my entire perspective while studying in school, then I could do the same in the corporate world. I had no idea what I was getting myself into, but I was sure that I was never going to lose what I'd learned and experienced, and that my new awareness, inner strength, and commitment to personal growth would allow me to learn with every opportunity and in every situation.

When I started my first job, I was ready for this new phase of life. I'd told myself that in order to really see if this environment was for me, I'd have to maintain the same mentality as everyone else around me. I remember in the first week of my job I told my boss that I wanted to learn from him everything it took to succeed in this company. From that point onward, he took me under his wing and trained me to be the next corporate superstar. In order to really fit in there, I had to put aside some of the things I valued the most, the first being my freedom. I no longer had the ability to really follow what my heart desired; I had to abide by the strict rules, regulations, and policies that this organization valued. I was told what I had to wear to work every day and how to interact with others in the office and with the clients. I was even told how to write e-mails and proposals in very professional language and how to speak from a script, not from my heart. I was no longer allowed to be creative. I had to follow the path that had been set out for me, fit within the box that had been built for my role, and not venture outside of it. Change simply took too long, and there would be too much resistance from those higher up in the company, so it was best to just do the work and not question anything. I could no longer be my *true* self. Instead, I had to create a new, professional, almost robotic version of myself. I had to put on a mask every day and pretend to be someone I wasn't. But if I followed what my superiors had set out for me, I'd make a lot of money, gain a lot of respect, and maybe even become a big player in the corporate world.

So every day I'd wake up early, put on a suit and tie (that I felt totally uncomfortable in), and join the crowds of people on the subway as we all commuted downtown. I'd sit at my desk without a window, produce my work in a voice and style that wasn't my own, and do as my boss told me. I'd party at night, going out with my friends and drinking to shake off the boredom that came with working in an uptight environment. I had joined the ranks of corporate (North) America, but I certainly wasn't fulfilled. I fell into an unconscious routine and lost touch with all the positive practices I'd been implementing while in school. I wasn't being coached by my father very frequently, and I wasn't even aware of how unhappy I was becoming. Life clearly had other plans for me though.

During this time, I experienced a profound moment just before my grandfather's unveiling ceremony (a tradition in the Jewish religion where the family of the deceased gathers in the cemetery six months to one year after the person dies to unveil the tombstone), which woke me up from my unconscious state of living. I was having a conversation with my dad in the cemetery about how uncomfortable I was feeling with certain things in my life. He suggested that maybe I had not adjusted to the working world as well as he thought. Since I hadn't been coaching with him as often, he had no idea how unhappy I truly was. When he suggested this, it stirred up all the feelings I had been repressing for the past few months. I was so shaken up that I decided to take a walk to process this. I found myself sitting on a bench, looking at a pond, and thinking, *How do I get out of this funk?* It was at that very moment that I saw a leaf fall from a nearby tree, flutter as if it were in slow motion, and land in the water. The ensuing ripple effect that the leaf created spread throughout the pond.

With everything in stillness around me, I felt stillness once again within, and it spoke to me. In that moment, I recognized I'd become so entranced by the idea of succeeding in the business world that I'd temporarily put aside all that had brought me happiness over the past few years. I realized that my ego had taken over, and I was no longer connected with my heart or my truth. From that point forward, I recommitted myself to my journey. I began coaching with my father again; meditating frequently; and practicing thinking, speaking, and acting in a loving and supportive way. I used the techniques I'd learned while in school and began applying them to this new phase of my life. What I'd learned about myself was now a part of me and would never leave. This wisdom could be applied and practiced in any situation, environment, or relationship.

After becoming aware of my truth once again, it was difficult to be happy in my work environment. My first reaction was to run. I immediately had the desire to quit, put my things in a backpack, and travel the world. I wanted to escape from the troubled routine I'd unconsciously created. I was convinced that traveling would allow me to find what I was truly meant to do with my life, since I knew I wouldn't be able to figure this out while trapped in a soulless corporate position.

However, just like in the other crises I'd experienced over the past three years, my father was there for support and to help me shift my perspective. He suggested that if I were to run away from this challenge, it would follow me wherever I went. After a bit of a struggle, I decided to stay in that job and work through the challenges I was experiencing. After all, I didn't want these lessons to keep coming back.

What You Resist Persists

Coined by Carl Jung, this phrase has come to be a huge part of my life. Back when I first learned this lesson, I realized that no matter how much a person or situation was bothering me, if I ran away (resist), it would come back and find me in another form (persist). For example, let's say that you have a boss whose controlling nature drives you nuts. While you desperately try to hold your own, express your opinions, and maintain a sense of freedom, he always seems to maintain the upper hand.

So you quit your job, assuming that you're now free from this person and his influence over you. You even decide to work for yourself to avoid letting another boss possess this power.

A few months later, you find yourself in a romantic relationship—and suddenly you're extremely unhappy but don't know why. When you step back to gain perspective

> on the situation, you realize that you're now subject to the same power hold you were experiencing in your last job. All this time, you've been resisting being controlled, and now you're in a romantic relationship with someone who's doing just that. What you resist persists. The more you fight giving up control, the more you attract controlling people into your life. Only when you can come to terms with the fear of losing control and realize that you have power over your life will this issue stop showing up. When you let go, life flows.

The greatest challenge I was facing was the fear of permanently losing my freedom. Since I'd begun this job, I felt as if I were constantly being told what I could and could not do. There was very little room to do what I wanted. Freedom was, and always will be, my number one value in life, and thus being in an environment that promoted very little individual discretion was extremely frustrating and draining. I was able to overcome this challenge by understanding that being free is much more than a physical place, thing, or experience; it is a mind-set that can be created within. I realized that I could feel liberated anywhere. The key lay in my perspective, the way I was thinking, and the choices I was making.

The second challenge was that my creativity had been stifled by the "in the box" attitude that my job was promoting. As I described in earlier chapters, I'd never done what others told me to do while growing up. Since I used to rebel against anyone who tried to control me, you can imagine how difficult it was for me to spend 45 hours a week in an environment where I had no choice but to do what I was told. I had no outlet to express myself in the workplace, and as a result, I was so drained by the time I got home that I had no energy for the other areas of my life.

To me, the corporate world felt very unnatural and robotic. I was afraid to show my feelings in this type of environment, and I found myself reverting back to what I had done as a kid: suppressing everything. For a sensitive person like me, this was not a welcoming place to be. Although I did a good job of pretending, I'd truly lost touch with my authentic self. I put so much effort into playing the game that I forgot who the real me was. The work culture required that I really separate my personal and professional lives. However, I spent so much time in professional mode that I lost touch with the part of me that was authentic, genuine, and ultimately happy. (See *Getting to Know Your True Self* in the Resources section.)

The beautiful thing about what I was going through was that my awareness was very strong. I became conscious of every one of my habits, actions, words, and thoughts, and how they were creating my unhappy life. I was empowered enough to know that if I were able to change things around during school, then I could most certainly do the same now. With my new awareness and empowered sense of self, I made myself a promise that I'd stay in my job until I felt I'd learned everything I was supposed to, so I could then comfortably move on to my next adventure with confidence.

The first place I looked to make a change in was my lifestyle both at the office and at home. I realized that it was full of routine, lacked flexibility, and was extremely boring. I decided to focus on what I could do outside of work first, so I could create more space for activities that promoted freedom. First, I began to incorporate the practices that had brought me great clarity, peace, and happiness while I was at university. I started meditating again, this time more frequently. I used my journal as an outlet to express myself through writing. I made sure I had time for mindful movement four to five times a week, including yoga and swimming. (See *Movement* in the Resources section.) I thought and spoke to myself with more kindness, encouragement, love, and respect. And I also used positive affirmations daily and reminded myself of all the things I was grateful for whenever I had a free moment.

Once I had my foundation back, I began to find ways to increase the amount of spontaneity in my life. I'd try to plan less and go with the flow more often. The groundwork that I'd once again laid eventually made its way into the workplace, and my days became more tolerable. The better I felt about myself, the more comfortable I felt expressing what I was feeling both inside and outside of the office. I realized that I no longer wanted to pretend to be someone else and slowly began to honor who I truly was.

I also started to share with my colleagues some of the philosophies and principles I'd learned and practiced over the years and found that they were really interested in hearing what I had to say. I even developed a close relationship with a few of them, whom I began coaching during lunches and coffee breaks. To help my spirit come to life in the office, I began whistling, humming, and singing while doing my work. I found creative ways of completing the same old tasks, making them more tolerable.

After slowly navigating my way through these challenges, I felt as if I'd learned all that I was supposed to from this job, and after a year decided it was time to move on. If I hadn't spent all those months working through the issues that came up while in that environment, I'm convinced that I wouldn't be where I am today, with the confidence in myself, my vision, and my purpose on this planet. I chose not to run but rather face my problems head-on. So when I finally quit, I was sure that life would bring me exactly what I needed.

I spent the next two years working as my own boss on various contracts and part-time gigs in a few different fields. On some level, I knew that I was getting ready for what life had in store for me next. I told myself that I was taking the time to figure out how to run my own business. I learned something new from each experience and applied it to the next one. I became enthralled with my own personal growth and evolution and spent what felt like every spare moment learning more about myself.

I soon realized that my passion was sharing all the wisdom I'd gained with other young people. I wanted to provide them with access to the information and resources that had helped me so much. I made it my goal to somehow offer support, encouragement, and inspiration to young people so they could start living with more happiness, optimism, self-worth, and passion. I wanted to let them know that all that they were looking for existed within them already, and that they were empowered to make choices that would create a life they were truly proud of. After all, so many kids needed to know that with every positive thought they think, loving word they speak, and kind action they show toward themselves and others, they're empowering themselves to make their dreams come true. This was my life vision, and I was just beginning to realize it.

Within two years of uncovering that vision, it had very much become a reality. In March 2010, I created an organization called the Youth Wellness Network with the intention of teaching these ideas and principles to young people all over the world. The organization grew quickly, as the programs began to positively impact many lives. I went through my breakdown at the age of 19, and if my dad hadn't been around to empower me to make positive changes, I don't know where I'd be today. I now help and empower young men and women in the same way my father assisted me. I am living my passion, my dream, and my truth, and I am on a journey to inspire and empower youth all over the world to join me in doing the same for themselves.

Jeffrey's Story

Since by now I'd come so far on my journey, I was honestly expecting life to be easier as I began to reap the rewards of my learning. It turns out I was wrong. While I did have the tools available to help me cope with what came next, they didn't make the challenges any less emotionally trying. You see, no matter how enlightened we think we are, the realities of life can still be overwhelming. The best we can hope for is the self-confidence and self-love to move through our trials and tribulations and come out in one piece. As I've become more self-aware, my experiences have become fuller and often more enjoyable, but still my greatest lessons come from my most difficult struggles.

From 2006 to 2008, a number of events unfolded that made my life extremely hard to endure at times. Thankfully, all the work I'd done allowed me to cope with these situations and eventually move into a more calm and peaceful space. But first I had a lot more learning to do.

Around the same time that I was beginning my journey of self-discovery, our business was undergoing some dramatic changes. We'd decided to open a new division and physical plant that I thought would help us grow and diversify. We put a significant amount of money into this expansion, but then struggled to make it work. Basically, I was never able to find the right person to grow this arm of the business, and as a result, it never took off. Even though I desperately held on to it for some time, not wanting to admit that I'd made a bad decision, we finally had to shut down the entire operation and take a huge financial hit. This was the first true failure I'd experienced in my career, and it felt pretty terrible. While I was eventually able to admit that I'd been wrong, what terrified me was the financial situation that this mistake had left me in. This brought up a lot of fears around money and not having enough for the future. (See *The Fear Pot* in the Resources section for a powerful exercise in overcoming your fears.)

Just prior to this, I'd entered into an agreement to purchase my brother's shares in the company, essentially buying him out. To make a long story short, with circumstances as they were now, I was no longer able to fulfill my end of the agreement and had to default on the buyout and give him back his shares.

I saw this as another failure, and it was a huge hit to my self-esteem. Suddenly, I began to question all of my decisions and wonder where I'd gone so wrong. For someone who once prided himself on success and perfection, I was suddenly coming up against a lot of failure in a short amount of time. While I tried to see the lessons in all of this, it was hard to be objective in the moment. I was extremely stressed out and unsure what my next move should be. Luckily, because I was working with a coach and spending a great deal of time on myself, I was able to cope much better than I would have in the past. I didn't get sick. I didn't have a breakdown. I tried to stay in the moment as much as possible, accepting my frustration and despair and allowing it to move through me.

I thought that in order for the business to bounce back, I'd have to work extremely hard to repair the damages I'd caused. But since I was no longer passionate about working full-time in my old capacity, I considered selling. I thought that letting it go might be my way out. So I entered into preliminary discussions with a personal friend and associate who'd shown an interest in the company. I'll never forget the meeting I had with him and our accountants. After reviewing our financial statements, he said, "Why would I want to buy this company? It will be broke in a few years." I was shocked and extremely hurt. This was the business I'd dedicated my entire adult life to building. *How can he say such things?* I thought. *Can he possibly be right?* Thankfully, he was wrong—the business is still around today, and although it's had its ups and downs, it's now on solid footing once again. But my ego was severely bruised after that meeting. I had a lot of emotions to process, and I had to forgive him in order to let myself move on.

The Power of Forgiveness

The ability to forgive is one of the most powerful tools that I've learned in my ten years as a coach. It isn't as much about the other person as it is about you. Forgiveness doesn't necessarily mean talking to the person who has wronged you and saying, "I forgive you," but rather doing that work internally to let go of the anger, hurt, and resentment and the control these feelings can have over you. While I couldn't change what that colleague said about our company, I could change the way I *felt* about his comment. Holding on to the anger and hurt would only bring *me* more pain and suffering—and, ironically, wouldn't impact him at all.

The truth is that the only person you hurt by not forgiving someone else is you. So in pardoning my friend, I was setting myself free. I was able to move on with my confidence intact. The only reason this was possible was because I'd already put so much work into loving myself and believing in my own self-worth. As Buddha said, "Holding on to anger is like grasping a hot coal with the intent of throwing it at someone else; *you* are the one who gets burned."

So I was back to the drawing board. I had to do what was best for the business and my own well-being. The manager we'd hired to run the company continued to work extremely hard and took on a significant leadership role. He built the business back up while I focused on my coaching practice. I loved the work I was doing now—helping other people and learning new things about myself along the way. While I knew this new venture wasn't going to make me rich, I did it because it made me feel good.

While things seemed to be improving professionally, I wasn't in the clear yet. There was more drama on the way that would send my entire family life into a tailspin. In January 2007, I was in the middle of a coaching session when I received a call from a hospital in Florida. My parents, who move to Florida every winter, had been in a terrible car accident. My father was in a coma, and my mother had a broken pelvis and severe bruising. Suddenly, I was making arrangements to fly down and be with them. Lois and I, along with my siblings, spent the next few weeks at my mother's side, helping her cope with the trauma and praying that my father would wake up.

Eventually, we were able to make arrangements to have them transferred back to Ottawa (where they lived the other half of the year). But after three weeks, my dad remained unresponsive, and we were forced to make the decision to remove the life-support tubes that were keeping him alive. Needless to say, my mother was devastated, and we were all in a state of shock. Sitting in the hospital room watching my father die, I realized what his purpose had been in my life, and I was able to forgive him, love him, and let him go. Following the funeral and seven-day *shiva,* where we were surrounded by family and friends, the next few months were spent helping my mom adjust to life on her own.

In 2008, things started to turn around, and our family was blessed with some great news. First, Hailey was engaged to be married, and shortly after that Allan proposed to his long-time girlfriend Natalie. We would have two weddings in five months—which was both a wonderful celebration for our family and a huge hit to my pocketbook. I tried to focus on the excitement and not worry about money, but obviously financial abundance was still an issue I needed to work on.

In addition to this news, all three of our kids were starting to build their lives in Toronto, so Lois put more pressure on me for us to move there, too. She'd been born and raised in the city, and had moved to Pembroke in 1979 after we were married. Now she wanted to go home and be in the same city as our children. I, on the other hand, had been born in a small town and spent most of my life there, so I was terrified of moving to Toronto. Even compared to Ottawa, it was quite overwhelming. I had no idea what kind of life we'd have. I started thinking, *How will I reestablish myself as a coach? Will we still be able to spend time in nature? Will we even be able to afford life there? How can I face the guilt if I leave my mother in Ottawa and move away?* I was extremely opposed to the idea, but the more I resisted, the more Lois pushed.

We started looking for a place to live in Toronto and put our condo in Ottawa on the market to see if it would sell. This was the beginning of a long and trying process that fortunately ended extremely well. Although our home in Ottawa didn't sell for more than two years, we found the place of our dreams in Toronto and made the move to be with our children. We let go of our fear of not having enough money and carried both condos for the time being. Finally, when we surrendered to faith, our condo in Ottawa sold, and we were freed of that financial burden.

In 2010, our daughter gave birth to a baby girl named Willow, and 17 months later our daughter-in-law Natalie gave birth to a baby boy named Theo. As our family grew, life got even more exciting. Now that I no longer had all the stress of providing for a growing family and trying to impress my parents at the same time, I was free to enjoy my grandchildren more than I had been able to enjoy my own kids when they were babies.

My granddaughter is now two, and I find that she really helps bring out my inner child. While my own kids would likely say that I didn't play with them much when they were young, and I've always been known as a serious person, I now find myself behaving in silly, childlike ways when she's around. Having grandchildren has opened me up to emotions and behaviors I never allowed myself to experience before. I believe it's really important for adults to remain in touch with this aspect of themselves. Just because you're grown up doesn't mean you have to be serious or responsible all the time. Letting your inner child out to play is extremely liberating and so good for your soul! These days, I feel freer and more at ease—and I'm able to really enjoy family time without all the stress and pressure I once felt.

I believe parents have a role to play in supporting and enabling their kids to grow and succeed, regardless of whether they're still young or grown adults. Now that my children are out on their own, I believe I have an even more vital role to play in their lives. I like to think of myself as a consultant who offers them advice, guidance, and a helping hand as they go through the experiences of being an adult.

I've been working with Michael for a long time, and just recently our relationship has undergone another transition. Now that he's become successful as a speaker, writer, teacher, and business owner, I pride myself on my ability to mentor and support him—and even learn from him. I truly cherish our relationship and am extremely proud of how successful he's become. I love the fact that we get to work together as coauthors, speakers, and teachers. I've always believed that Michael would be able to carve out his own path and do some of the things I wish I'd done when I was younger. I support his decision to go where others haven't gone and avoid conforming to what they may have expected of him. I know he and I will continue to play a big role in each other's lives, because we share similar beliefs and a common passion for helping to inspire and empower others. I am proud to be Michael's father and glad to be not only his coach and mentor, but, most important, his friend.

The Power to Empower Others

One of the most inspiring things I've learned since becoming a coach is that once I was able to take responsibility for my own life, I could then hold the space for others to do the same. This realization has changed my relationship with all of my children. I believe that if more parents encouraged their kids to take personal responsibility for their lives, more young people would grow up empowered and inspired rather than rebellious and disillusioned.

I now understand that there were many things I could have done differently while my children were growing up that would have led to a more peaceful relationship and home environment. Many adults like me underestimate the power and wisdom of young people, believing that since they don't know better they must be controlled. As a parent, I spent so much time trying to prevent my kids from experiencing the same pain and discomfort I lived through by telling them what to do, how to do it, and when to do it. But in trying to protect them, I realize now that I was actually causing more harm than good. In deciding everything for them, I was actually disempowering them from making healthy choices on their own. I was setting them up for a lifetime of indecisiveness and powerlessness. I now know that it doesn't have to be that way!

Once children's primary needs are met (love, food, and shelter), and they're safe from physical harm, parents then have the opportunity to allow their kids the freedom to become personally responsible. In allowing your young ones to think and act for themselves, and then respecting their decisions, you'll move to a place of trust, love, and faith. All of these experiences will let them learn, grow, and make mistakes. The more you have faith that life will bring them exactly what they need, when they need it, the more they'll be able to gain the self-knowledge required to flourish as adults. You just have to trust that no matter what they go through, they'll become more evolved people as a result.

This doesn't mean you *shouldn't* be a parent to your children—quite the contrary. It's just a shift in the way you take on this role by default. For example, you can still provide guidance and share your own stories, but you must own these as yours, not as things that might or will happen to your kids. You can teach them that actions always have consequences, and the more aware they are of these consequences, the easier their choices become. You can show them how to make decisions that truly feel good within them, and then to live with and learn from the repercussions, no matter what they are. You can share your own morals and values while encouraging them to create their own. You can teach them that the more they're able to respect and love themselves, the more they'll be able to respect and love others. If more parents are able to accomplish all this, it's possible that the next generation will grow up feeling more in control of their lives and more personally responsible for the realities they're manifesting.

While I unconsciously spent a lot of time controlling Michael as a young person—telling him what to do, forcing him to behave a certain way around the house, and pressuring him to act maturely in the classroom and in public—I realize now that I didn't set him up for success.

When he finally moved away from home to live on his own at university, he was unable to confidently make decisions for himself, and as a result, he struggled tremendously. Only when he started working with me in a coaching relationship did I learn the value of allowing him (with my support) to take complete responsibility for himself. As a coach, I didn't tell Michael what to do, and I never provided solutions for his problems and concerns. Rather, I empowered him to look within and realize how much control he actually had over the events transpiring in his life.

This isn't just true for parents and children. I believe that it's in all of our best interests to give all the people in our lives—spouses, siblings, employees, students, friends, and so on—the space to make their own choices and learn from their mistakes. If you're able to release the desire to control every outcome and tell others what to do, they'll be free to grow into unique, confident people.

The more that we allow each other to live personally responsible lives, the more harmonious our relationships and environments will become. We'll all thrive if given the chance to do so.

The most efficient way to encourage others to take ownership of their own lives is to lead by example. The more we move from a "do as I say" to a "do as I do" approach, the more enabled individuals will be to make happier, healthier, and more positive choices that feel good to them.

Empowerment and personal responsibility are the way of the future. Through these practices, young leaders will be nurtured and supported. And this next generation will have the opportunity and the ability to repair our planet and live in peace.

While I spent a great deal of time studying theories of empowerment, change, and personal growth throughout my journey, the greatest transformations in my life came when I engaged fully in the challenges life dealt me. No matter how difficult, I knew that if I didn't experience these trials, I wouldn't grow as a person. Eventually, I put away the books, CDs, and DVDs and started learning experientially. I applied all the knowledge I had obtained and made it work for me as I continued to be tested. You see, when carbon undergoes tremendous pressure and increased heat over an extended period of time, a diamond is formed. At times that's what my life felt like. I needed all of these trying circumstances to push me outside of my comfort zone and force me to learn and grow and flourish. I can't say that I enjoyed the sad and difficult experiences I lived through during those years, but deep down I recognized them for what they were—the most valuable lessons life could hand me.

Chapter Seven

DREAMS REALLY
DO COME TRUE

Michael's Story

The past two years have been quite the ride. Since starting the Youth Wellness Network, life has taken me in a wonderful new direction that's been overflowing with many deeply fulfilling circumstances and heart-opening relationships. Each one has given me an opportunity to integrate important lessons in a more profound way.

In the spring of 2010, just before I started the Youth Wellness Network, I was in the midst of an intense learning experience that involved another youth-focused venture I'd begun with a business partner. We spent eight months working closely on a project that involved bringing wellness events to universities, but then hit a roadblock that resulted in the breakdown of our professional relationship and our business. The entire situation left me quite shaken up. This was technically the first company I'd ever been involved in founding, and it was the closest I'd come to working on something aligned with my passion.

Although this was a heart-wrenching experience, it proved to be a gift in that it allowed me to become clearer on what I wanted. After things fell apart, I spent two weeks in an intense reflective state, journaling, meditating, and coaching with my dad. Throughout this process, he urged me to look beyond just running an organization that helped empower youth, and instead to map out how I saw my life as a whole unfolding. This vision would be the impetus I needed to create the Youth Wellness Network.

What Is a Life Vision?

A life vision is a road map or a set of guiding principles that, if followed, will help you transform your passions and dreams into reality. The process of creating a life vision not only allows you to become clear on what you truly want, but also helps those things take shape and find their way into existence. It's the key to putting all of your learning into action, and it nudges you to move from a place of understanding to one of practice.

The first step in creating my life vision was to understand what I truly wanted. By working with my dad, I realized that my desires lay beneath the surface. I've found that many people tend to focus solely on their superficial aspirations (for example, the new car, the important job title, the perfect marriage) and confuse these with their true desires (happiness, fulfillment, love, and so on). So when they do get the things they thought they wanted, they don't experience the results or feelings they were looking for.

Personally, I thought that all I desired was a business that would help empower youth, but I realized that what I really wanted was to feel free, fulfilled, helpful, authentic, empowered, and understood. That didn't mean I wasn't supposed to start this organization, it just meant that whatever I was going to do next had to be perfectly aligned with these core feelings. I was aware at the time that my true passion and purpose was sharing with youth the practices, principles, and strategies that had helped me create a happier and healthier life. But how I was actually going to accomplish this remained a mystery. I decided to put my focus on allowing my emotions to guide me into action, and then pledged that if I didn't feel the way I ultimately wanted to, I'd change what I was doing or how I was doing it.

As I moved forward with the process of creating my life vision, I noticed that I had a tendency of trying to figure everything out before it actually happened. This was rooted in my fear of the unknown. Because of this apprehension, I tried to control as much as I possibly could and refused to trust anyone else to do what needed to be done. One of the reasons why my previous venture had fallen apart was because I was unable to let go of this need to dominate the project. I'd fallen into the habit of focusing on all the goals I wanted to accomplish based on a very rigid time line rather than allowing my journey to unfold organically. I realized that the key facet of the life-vision process I wasn't yet practicing was trust. I didn't yet believe that the Universe would guide me to exactly where I needed to be when I needed to be there. As soon as I learned this lesson and began to make it a part of my life, things changed almost instantaneously.

Life isn't about the final destination or the accomplishments and accolades; it's about the journey and the opportunities for learning—and how we grow as a result. I'm not saying that effort isn't required, but that effort must be put toward actions rather than outcomes. It's not about how we're going to get somewhere, but what we *do* each step of the way.

So in May 2010, I set out to put these new insights into practice. As I moved forward in building the Youth Wellness Network, I used each experience as a chance to reprogram an old way of operating. Once I was clear on my vision, I decided to share it with whoever was willing to listen. One of my old beliefs had been: *When you have a good idea, don't share it because someone will take it.* I decided that this no longer made me feel good or served me in any way. So I swapped it for: *The more I share my vision with others, the more these ideas will grow and become a reality.* Another new belief I decided to live by was: *The size of the active network base with whom I maintain positive relationships directly correlates with my overall well-being.* I realized that the more I connected with new, interesting, and inspiring people; shared my ideas with anyone willing to listen; and trusted the Universe to show me the way, the faster everything would unfold. It was remarkable. What started out as a simple idea was growing into a full-blown organization.

Only a few months into starting the Youth Wellness Network I found myself in a room full of health-and-wellness administrators and professionals at the University of Toronto. Although they loved my vision, they wanted a more specific action plan—something I had not yet developed. They advised me to create a specific program that I could run at the university and then pitch it to them. My immediate thought was: *How will I ever be able to do this in such a short period of time and all on my own?*

Luckily, I was already used to living from the journey and vision mentality, so I set the intention to create my first program, trusted I'd be guided throughout the process, and let go of trying to figure out *how* it would come to fruition. The next week I sat down with one of my mentors, and by the end of the conversation our collaborative energy had helped me create my first program: The Break Zone. Within two months, I had a commitment from the university to pilot this program on their campus in the upcoming school year. I'd bring together a variety of wellness practitioners to work on-site during the exam period and offer free services to students, including laughter therapy, sound healing, and meditation.

The program was so successful that it caught the attention of a local high school. At the time, I was convinced that I was supposed to work with the 18- to 25-year-old demographic (which I was still a part of), and I hadn't even thought about the high-school market. But it seemed that life was taking me in a different direction once again. I got back in touch with my core feelings and let them lead the way. I released my attachment to the "how," and instead of fighting against this new direction, I decided to trust that I was being steered down a path that was aligned with my highest good.

Shifting from Goals to Intentions

An essential step in creating your life vision is setting intentions for the things you would like to experience. This is not nearly as definitive or structured as setting goals. *Intentions* give you the opportunity to make alterations and corrections to your path as you go. *Goals* are more rigid and promote getting to a specific destination in a specific way. Your life vision is a loose template of where you're heading. By setting intentions, your focus shifts away from the endgame toward the experiences, feelings, and learning you encounter along the way. Intentions allow you to stay open to the many possibilities that can lead to your desired outcome.

The more I grew my network and established new relationships, the more I encountered new opportunities to share my vision. A dream I'd had for many years was to one day work with Hay House. I'd attended numerous I Can Do It! conferences with my family, read many books by Hay House authors, and believed strongly in the mission of this company. But the idea of writing a book had never crossed my mind. Instead, my desire was to introduce their inspiring catalog of resources to a younger audience.

Through a family friend named Evelyne Banks, I was given the opportunity to connect directly with Hay House's event director, Nancy Levin. I sent her an e-mail proposing that Hay House become a sponsor of the Youth Wellness Network programs. While she wasn't able to commit to my proposal at the time, she offered me a complimentary ticket to an upcoming event called Movers

& Shakers that they were putting on in Toronto. Led by *New York Times* best-selling author Cheryl Richardson and Hay House CEO and president Reid Tracy, the event was intended for aspiring speakers and authors looking to reach a larger audience with their work. This was not the response I had been looking for, but I shifted my perspective and accepted her generous offer with gratitude.

As the event approached, I was uncertain as to what I'd get out of it. I didn't really fit into the demographic I thought they were looking for, and I was even a bit skeptical. I did, however, feel as though meeting new people and having more opportunities to share my vision could possibly open more doors. I had no idea just how big a door I was about to open.

When I arrived at the convention center for the first session of the three-day workshop, I went straight to the restroom. To my delight, I bumped into Louise Hay. I hadn't been expecting to see her there, as it wasn't advertised anywhere that she'd be in attendance. I expressed my gratitude to her for inviting me to the event and told her how much her books, movies, and affirmations had helped me throughout my journey. This was a great moment for me, as it was such an honor to meet her, and it also provided me with confirmation that I was truly supposed to be there.

The beautiful thing about creating a life vision is that if you're paying attention, life will send you subtle messages that confirm you're heading in the right direction. They can show up in many different ways, shapes, sizes, and forms, so the more aware you are in each moment, the easier it is to recognize the message. For me, seeing Louise Hay walk out of the restroom and having the opportunity to introduce myself was a clear sign that I was indeed on the right path.

That evening when I got home, a voice inside told me to post a link to the Youth Wellness Network on Cheryl Richardson's Facebook page. Since I'd spent many years learning to trust that voice, I did what I was told. The next day, about halfway through the morning session, one of the attendees mentioned an interest in working with young people. Cheryl spoke up, asking who the person was who'd posted a link about young people on her Facebook wall the night before. I responded by confidently raising my hand. She then praised me for the work I was doing and mentioned how she thought my story was very compelling. Needless to say, I was beyond thrilled to be recognized by such an accomplished author and speaker!

During the next break, I was surrounded by more than 30 individuals, all wanting to know more about me and what I was doing. I had some really great conversations and met some very nice people who shared common intentions to work with youth. The best part was that I felt truly ready for all the recognition I was receiving. I'd spent so much time becoming clear on what I wanted, setting intentions, and letting go of trying to figure out *how* it was all going to happen. As a result, I wasn't surprised by all the doors that were opening for me; I finally felt as if I'd arrived.

That same day after lunch, I decided to go up and talk to Louise. I felt a strong urge to share more about my vision with her, and that same voice inside my head said that she would be supportive. Instantly, I felt a strong, almost motherly connection with her. We only had a few minutes to chat, so I quickly told her my story and a bit about the work I was doing with youth. I also asked if I could have her e-mail address to send her more information. I was beyond thrilled when she said yes.

This weekend event proved to be a profound experience for me and, on many levels, was the confirmation I needed to continue pursuing my dreams. It took a great deal of courage, commitment, persistence, and faith to create my own path and live my vision. When the doubts surfaced, I made a conscious choice to embrace rather than resist them. I kept fear at bay by focusing on my intention to empower youth and my faith that it would all unfold at the perfect time and in the ideal way.

Over the next four months, I sent Louise a few e-mails about the Youth Wellness Network and the work I was doing. This experience tested my belief and patience, as I never got a response from her. I knew deep within that I'd soon be working with Hay House, and it was a challenge to let go of trying to figure out *how* it would come about and in what capacity. What helped me through this feeling of limbo was the reminder that the only things I had control over were my own choices. I put all my energy and focus into growing the Youth Wellness Network, and I knew that when the timing was right the door to Hay House would open without me having to push it. Finally, after four months, I received a response from Louise. She expressed to me that it had been a passion of hers to work with kids for some time. She also shared that Hay House was looking to bring on younger teachers in order to reach younger audiences and was wondering if I'd be interested. Of course, I responded with a resounding *yes!*

The next few months continued to test my patience, but I kept responding with more trust and faith. I wasn't going to allow my fear of the unknown to rule my world anymore. I now had high schools approaching me to work with them, opportunities to run more workshops with youth groups, and even some requests to do inspirational speaking to larger audiences. All the while, I continued to reevaluate my wants and intentions.

As new opportunities came in, I'd check in to see if they were going to help fulfill the core feelings I desired. I'd then decide whether to pursue the opportunity or let it go. This is how I developed the ability to discern. *Discernment* is a very important step in living your life vision. Once your intentions begin to bring about results, you need to learn how to sift through them to determine which ones will be of benefit to you and which ones will not.

As favorable circumstances continued to flow into my life, I realized that I had to alter my intentions slightly, since they were no longer the same as when I started the organization. My vision had grown, and my heart was being led to something more expansive where I could inspire larger groups of youth, parents, and teachers. I put the lesson of discernment into practice and learned to say no to opportunities that didn't immediately feel right.

One Sunday morning in the spring of 2011, my inner voice strongly urged me to e-mail Louise with an update of all the wonderful things that were unfolding for me. Within an hour of sending it, I got a response from her. She was thrilled to hear of my progress and was also excited to share the news that she was ready to discuss the possibility of working on a project to reach young people. So we set up a time to meet at an upcoming I Can Do It! conference in Toronto.

Over the next couple of months leading up to our meeting, I spent very little time thinking about what this project would look like. I knew that if I let myself go into that space, my head would begin to take over and I'd try to figure it all out before it even began. Therefore, I put all my effort and focus back into what I was presently working on. I stayed true to my vision and intentions and released any attachment to a specific outcome.

The morning of our meeting, I felt a wide range of emotions. There were definitely some nerves and excitement, but overall I felt quite calm and centered. I kept reminding myself, *All will continue to unfold for my highest and best good, and I will embrace everything that life brings me with an open mind and an open heart.* As I walked into the room, I was greeted with a big hug from Louise, who is definitely one of the best huggers in the world. We spent the next 20 minutes or so chatting about life, and it was such a wonderful experience to feel that motherly energy from her once again.

Soon after, Reid Tracy joined us and we got down to business. I was given an opportunity to share with them my vision for the Youth Wellness Network and all the positive change I knew I was here to facilitate in the lives of youth. Then I heard my inner voice nudge me to mention an idea my dad and I had recently discussed that involved the two of us working together to empower both parents and young people. Reid was interested, and by the end of our conversation what had started out as an idea for a weekend workshop became the outline for this very book. Walking into that meeting, I had no idea that writing a book would be the next step in allowing my vision to become a reality. But by the time I walked out, it was clear that's what I was supposed to do.

I could have easily gone into a state of panic when it dawned on me that neither my dad nor I had ever written anything longer than a newsletter. Instead, I put my positive affirmations to work, embracing what life brought me and trusting the direction I was being guided to go in.

This is the beautiful thing about living a life vision: if you truly let go of how it's all going to unfold, you have the ability to be flexible and go with the flow. If I'd stuck with the plan that my logical side had laid out for me, and had remained focused on not only what I wanted but how I was going to get there, I would have missed the opportunity to be a published author. This book is the result of my commitment to living my life vision.

Take a moment and ask yourself: *Am I experiencing the life I have always wanted, or am I stuck in someone else's dream?* I created my own path because I was tired of a life that wasn't my own. Hopefully my story will inspire you to realize that by creating and living your own life vision, anything is possible and dreams really *do* come true.

Back in 2010 when the idea for the Youth Wellness Network came to me, I knew that I had finally started to live the most empowered version of myself. No longer was I going to let society dictate how I lived or how I achieved success. I broke free from all the beliefs and constraints that had been holding me back, and I stepped into my own greatness. My dad was there by my side throughout the process, and I owe much of my empowerment to him. Through his actions, his willingness to change, and his desire to lead the way, he proved that he no longer subscribed to the "do as I say, not as I do" mentality. He took a leap, and I followed.

Today, I'm happier, healthier, and more fulfilled than I ever thought possible. I'm now walking the talk, always committed to being a student of life and a teacher of what I live. I am on a life-long crusade to live the empowered *me* and pave the way for youth around the world to do the same.

Afterword

LIVING THE
EMPOWERED YOU

We hope that this book has provided you with the resources and inspiration you'll need to begin your own journey of self-discovery and empowerment. As you start to live the empowered you, you'll experience great changes and notice your life unfolding in exciting and unexpected ways. As this empowered version of yourself, you'll not only begin to experience all that life has to offer, but also serve as a role model and inspiration for others to follow suit.

If you're a parent, a teacher, or anyone who has daily interactions with youth, this is your chance to start implementing the "do as I do" mentality. The best way to inspire and empower others is to lead by example. Thank you for joining us in our mission to live an empowered life and provide the next generation with the tools to do the same. What follows are just some of the incredible changes you can expect as your journey unfolds. . . .

Every once in a while, you'll likely find yourself reflecting on how far you've come and how much has changed. It will no longer seem as important to dwell on what you *should* still achieve, but instead you'll have a much greater appreciation for what you've already accomplished. You'll look at the challenges you've faced as great learning experiences rather than causes of discomfort. And what you once considered failures will now be understood as necessary for lifelong learning.

Although you'll still have some moments of chaos, most often you'll be filled with inner calm. When you experience times of confusion and frustration, you'll be able to move more quickly to a sense of clarity. You'll no longer be afraid of the unknown. While you'll still be curious about how life will unfold, you'll be more comfortable allowing it to happen at its own pace. You'll become more flexible and spontaneous, not having to live with the rigidity you once relied on. You'll have slowed down your thoughts and learned to listen to them, and the ones that do come up on a regular basis will be far more positive and reassuring. Your power to choose thoughts that serve you well will influence your overall way of living.

You'll be much more connected to your feelings—experiencing and expressing them as they come up—and you'll realize how much fuller your life can be as a result. You'll laugh freely, cry openly, and enjoy your days with passion and excitement. You'll grant yourself permission to experience whatever emotion comes up, whether it feels good or not. Because you're more in touch with your emotions, you'll know how to express them in a healthy way. You will still encounter frustration, anger, and stress, but now they'll move through you with ease, causing much less harm. You'll embrace the fact that you can't predict how you're going to feel in the future, and instead focus only on what you're experiencing in the moment.

You'll no longer panic when you're feeling down. You'll realize that in this lower and slower state of energy fears may surface, which give way to negative thoughts. The difference will be that now you'll know with certainty that this too shall pass. Instead of being alarmed or acting irrationally, you'll explain to those who you interact with that you're feeling grumpy or tired or sad and that you're sorry in advance if you do or say anything that offends them.

You'll no longer have such a great desire to be right. You'll choose not to argue simply to prove your point, and when you do find yourself in an argumentative state, you'll understand that it's coming from the low energy that you're experiencing in the moment. You won't feel guilty, because you'll understand that you're human. You'll have given up the desire to be perfect, since you'll be so much more accepting of yourself as you are. And you'll no longer heap judgment upon yourself or others; you'll embrace your vulnerability and allow yourself to live fully.

You'll have overcome your fears so they no longer paralyze you. And, while there will still be times that fears present themselves, you'll be comfortable with them and know how to send them on their way. You'll take personal responsibility for yourself and everything in your life. You'll no longer need to make excuses or blame others when things don't go your way. You'll have patience when events don't happen as you expected them to, knowing that some things just aren't meant to be. You'll know that *life* is watching out for your well-being and has your best interests at heart.

You'll have come to truly practice the art of self-care. You'll know, fully, that you're the most important person in your world, and you'll practice this belief daily. You'll eat well; exercise often; and care for your physical, mental, emotional, and spiritual well-being. You'll feel so much more complete as a person, and others will take notice. They will ask you how you've changed and will want to know what your secret is. The people who used to bother you no longer will. While they likely won't have changed, your perception of them will be different. All of your relationships will be stronger and more secure—especially the one you have with yourself. You'll know so much about yourself that you never did before.

You'll have the incredible inner confidence of a child. You'll no longer feel the need to please others. When you do decide to do something for someone else, it won't be out of obligation, but because you want to do it. You'll live in a way that's authentic and genuine. You'll realize how many masks you used to hide behind that you no longer need. It won't matter to you if you're liked by others; you'll like yourself enough. You'll be able to give and receive equally well, and you'll feel more appreciative and grateful for all you have.

You'll have more time to do the things you enjoy. Even when you're busy, you won't feel rushed or overwhelmed, as you'll be dedicated to maintaining balance and prioritizing your obligations in a very conscious way. You'll find it much easier to say no to people in a loving and polite way, and you won't feel bad doing so, because you'll know that the more you take care of yourself, the more energy and love you'll have to offer others. You'll feel comfortable creating boundaries so as not to become too stressed or overworked.

Although you'll take action, it will no longer seem forced. You'll have energy like you've never had before, and when you do feel tired, you'll give yourself the time and space to recuperate. You'll navigate through life with ease and comfort. You'll see things from a different perspective, and you'll constantly be building new beliefs from this newfound clarity. You'll no longer see things in shades of gray, but rather in vibrant colors. Even a cloudy or dull day will seem more vibrant. You'll be more understanding of others, so that when someone does something that appears to be mean or selfish, you'll look for the reason behind this behavior.

You'll feel confident in your own views and no longer feel pressured to go along with what others claim to be true. You'll come to appreciate that the truth is not constant, but something that changes from person to person. You'll know for certain that you get to choose what your truth is. You'll freely shift old paradigms to ensure that your beliefs and values feel good to you.

By opening your heart, you'll feel things at a much deeper level. You'll allow your emotions to guide you forward, and your mind will follow. You'll work to keep your yin and yang energies in balance. You will believe that life is a journey and, instead of focusing on a particular destination, will enjoy the process of getting there.

From this new state of being, you'll find yourself becoming more conscious and aware. Opportunities will begin to turn up that defy logical explanation. More coincidences will occur, and you'll have confidence that these are beyond just good luck or good timing. You'll be far more aware of all your senses, and even find yourself developing a sixth sense or intuition. You'll be more willing to trust this guidance and allow it to direct your actions and decisions. You'll now know that things are not always as they seem.

As you continue to move to higher and higher levels of consciousness, you'll have moments when your mind is completely still and your heart is completely open. In the present moment, you'll begin to feel a connection to a magical force or energy that's still beyond your comprehension. You won't feel afraid of this energy—you'll be wowed by its apparent power.

There will be times when you're perfectly calm and able to turn entirely inward. In these moments, you'll experience a deep sense of peace, tranquility, calm, harmony, serenity, oneness, totality, and love. Even words will not properly describe what you're sensing in this moment, and once you've been there, you'll know that you can come back to this place to visit as often as you choose. If your connection to this magical force or energy is strong enough, you'll come to realize that all you've been desperately seeking is already within you. You no longer have to search or seek or push; instead, you'll just have to become totally present and know that it is so. As you relax, surrender, and let go of expectations and attachments, you'll recognize that you are powerful beyond your wildest dreams. You'll begin to comprehend that all your desires can come to fruition when you know that you are worthy of creating them. You will understand that it is you—and only you—who creates your life.

The *Empowered YOU* will know that *anything* is possible!

RESOURCES

You have now made it to the Resources section of this book—welcome! We've created it to help solidify the learning we've shared and guide you to turn it into practice and, hopefully, habit. The resources are divided into sections, which are made up of some of the principles that we believe are necessary for creating lasting change in your life.

We've included exercises, activities, and practices that you can make part of your daily routine or turn to when you're in a pinch. They function well individually or in conjunction with one another. Sometimes you'll want to work through them on your own, and other times you may want to involve your parent, child, or partner. In order to bring about change, repetition is required. The more you practice, the more natural these exercises will feel, and the more change you'll start to notice in your life.

Principle 1: Your Thoughts Create Your Reality

As we explained throughout the book, the thoughts you think influence the feelings you have, the responses they generate, and the way your life plays out as a result. Your thoughts are much more powerful than you may realize, and in order to put them to good use, you first need to slow them down, become aware of what they actually are, and then learn to shift them to focus on more positive and useful things.

Practice: Meditation

The first step in connecting with your thoughts is to slow them down. This is easier said than done. We've found meditation to be the best way to do so, but the very idea of meditating can be frightening to some people.

There are a wide range of techniques available, but what's most important is to find one that works for you. It must feel comfortable and easy or you won't want to do it on a regular basis. Even if you simply sit quietly in your chair, close your eyes, and focus on your breath, that's still a form of meditation. So remember to be easy on yourself at first.

The challenge with any meditative practice is that we often try to use our minds to figure out how to do it. This just makes it more difficult, because it's the mind we want to disengage. One of our favorite concepts comes from Albert Einstein, and states that no problem can be solved with the same mind-set that was used to create it. So developing a meditation practice that doesn't involve much thinking has a far greater chance of being successful than spending your time figuring out how to best meditate. Ensure that your method feels good for you, and don't worry about getting it right. When it comes to meditation, there's no right or wrong way. As long as you're quieting your mind, feeling calm, and becoming more present, then it's working.

Tips to Begin Your Meditation Practice:

- Find a quiet place with little to no distractions.

- Make sure you're comfortable (sitting or lying down, whichever feels better).

- Close your eyes.

- Play soft music or a guided-meditation audio program if this helps you.
- Focus on your breathing (breathe in through your nose and out through your mouth).
- Use stomach breathing (try to imagine each breath coming in through your diaphragm).
- As thoughts pop into your head, gently let them go or picture them as clouds floating away.
- Repeat this practice as often as you can.

Sample Meditative Practice:

Sit somewhere quiet, and use your breath to slow down your body and mind.

Start by putting your hand on your stomach, and focus your attention on breathing into this area.

Watch your belly expand and contract with every inhalation and exhalation. Breathe in through your nose and out through your mouth, nice and slow and as deeply as you can.

Let out a big, peaceful sigh on your next exhalation: *Ahh!*

Now try closing your eyes and breathing in this way at least ten times.

Some people prefer guided meditations to help direct their minds toward silence and stillness. If you are looking for a guided meditation to help with your practice, you can purchase and download Jeffrey's *Awakening the Self* meditation audio program here: **http://awakeningtheself.com/meditation-cd/**.

Practice: Daily-Thoughts Journal

Now that you've successfully quieted your mind, or are in the process of learning to do so, the next step is to become aware of the thoughts that are floating through your head on a daily basis. It's said the average person has between 50,000 and 80,000 thoughts per day. Unfortunately, a lot of these come from the unconscious mind, and we aren't even aware that we're having them. What has helped us draw attention to our thoughts and sort through them is the free-flow journaling process.

For five to ten minutes a day, whether it's in the morning or before you go to bed, find time to sit and write down all the thoughts that pop into your head, either in that moment or that you remember from the course of the day. Don't worry about grammar, spelling, or punctuation. There are no rules when writing in your journal. This is your sacred space, and anything goes. Try not to concern yourself with the experiences you had, but focus more on what you are, or were, thinking. Even if you start to consider how silly doing this is, write *that* down. This practice helps you to become more aware of your thoughts, and it also helps to empty them from your mind, since once they've been committed to paper, you've released them and no longer have to hold on to them.

Practice: Observing Your Thoughts

Many people find it helpful to practice being the observer of their own thoughts. Once you've developed a meditation practice to slow down your mind and emptied your thoughts into a journal in order to help decrease the amount you have per day, it will be easier to observe them and then change them into more positive ones. There are three exercises that have worked for us, making it possible to observe the thoughts in our heads.

1. *Calling out your thoughts.* As you become aware of a negative thought in your mind, simply say, "Negative," out loud. Depending on where you are, you may have to whisper it to yourself. The key is to bring awareness to it. You may be surprised by how many you have in one day. Once you're more comfortable identifying your negative thoughts, then you can begin to practice substituting them and train your mind to shift to something more positive instead.

2. *The elastic band.* This practice is not for everyone, but it can be effective in some situations. Put an elastic band around your wrist like a bracelet. Every time you catch yourself thinking a negative or limiting thought, gently snap the elastic band on your wrist. This will create awareness in your body that the negative thought creates discomfort. By doing this, you're training not only your mind, but also your body, to react a certain way when you're thinking negatively. Once you've got the hang of it, start to replace these thoughts with positive ones.

3. *Thinking about nothing.* This one might be a bit trickier for some people. Find a watch or clock with a second hand. The objective is to stare at and focus only on the second hand to see how many ticks you can go through without thinking about anything. Even if the thought pops up about how silly this exercise is, or how slowly the second hand is moving, that still counts as a thought. Every time you have a thought, start again. This practice will slowly train your mind to go longer and longer without any thoughts flowing through, and it also helps with reaching a state of stillness. Be kind to yourself throughout this process. When we first started, it was hard to get past one or two seconds without a thought. The more you practice, the easier it will become. Patience is very important for this one.

Principle 2: Express, Don't Suppress, Your Emotions

As we explained in the book, it's important to express your emotions (positive and negative) as they come up. If you hold on to them for too long, they can turn into disease or discomfort within the body or may build up to the point that you explode—thus expressing them in an unhealthy way. Happy or sad, let it out! Here are a few practices that we've found helpful.

Practice: Anger Release

Through our experience, we've learned that the best way to ensure that anger doesn't become too great or overpowering is to express it as soon as it comes up rather than trying to suppress or hide it. Here are some techniques that we've used:

— *Punch a pillow!* Find a pillow—and the bigger it is, the better. Form a fist with one or both of your hands, and hit the pillow with as much force as is required to let your anger out. Repeat this until you no longer feel the need to. A sense of calmness is a sign that the emotion has passed through you. You can also take the pillow and hit it against other pillows or something that won't break, like a bed or a wall. If you have access to a punching bag, this can also be useful, but make sure to protect your hands before you begin.

— *Scream!* Lock yourself in a car or a place where you won't disturb anyone. Then take a deep breath, and scream as loud as you can. You can say words or just make noise. Stop when you no longer feel any anger. Most likely, the anger will have passed through you and you can return to your day after a few breaths and screams.

Feel free to get creative with these forms of expression. Use whatever you have lying around the house. The most important thing is that you aren't harming yourself or anyone else in the process. It also helps if you don't break anything!

Practice: Laughter Therapy

Laughter is a wonderful way of expressing emotion and allowing whatever you're feeling to flow through you. We've found that although you may not feel like you're in the mood, laughing anyway will help you release your emotion or express it in a healthy way.

One way of bringing about laughter is to view funny videos or movies. If you have a favorite comedy, sit down and watch a few scenes. As much as you try to resist, before you know it you'll be cracking up without even knowing why. Through laughter, everything tends to become less serious: challenges dissolve faster and solutions are found effortlessly.

Another way to embrace this practice is through laughter yoga. If you search online, you'll most likely find a local wellness center that holds laughter-yoga sessions or an independent practitioner who runs workshops. This is a wonderful modality that can help you learn to laugh for no reason. The more you do it, the easier it becomes. And the easier it becomes, the more you're able to laugh on your own without assistance!

Practice: Art Therapy

Using art as an outlet to express your emotion is incredibly helpful. Whether you enjoy art or don't care for it at all, it can be therapeutic to pick up a crayon or marker and just draw. Don't think about it. Don't plan it. Just create! Even if it's just scribbles, it will help bring out your inner child and allow the emotion to flow. If you're angry, sometimes it helps to push harder on the crayon or move it faster across the page. Try not to judge or analyze what you're doing. Draw as if you are a child, and watch as the magic starts to happen and the emotion flows.

Practice: Music Therapy

Using sound or music as a way to express your emotion is a wonderful tool. No matter if you play music or simply listen to it, the effect can be the same. Have you ever noticed that when you're feeling sad you're drawn to sad songs? Or when you're angry you listen to more aggressive songs, and when you're happy you listen to upbeat, positive ones? This is your instinct helping to connect you to that specific emotion so it can move through you. If the music brings on tears, laughter, or the urge to dance, just go with it and let the emotion flow.

Practice: Writing or Journaling

The writing process can also help with releasing and expressing emotions in a healthy way. Similar to the drawing process, grab a pen and a notebook and just let your hand move across the page, writing whatever comes out. There's no need to think about what you're saying and no need to adhere to grammar or style rules; just put down what you're feeling without any restrictions. A helpful trick may be to pen a letter to someone and express what you're feeling, regardless of whether it's anger, sadness, or happiness. Once you've written it all down, take a big breath in and let it out. Then rip up the letter. This is a fantastic way of letting the emotion pass.

Practice: Movement

Finding a way to move your body in a healthy way is an incredible practice that allows you to express your emotion in a more physical manner. Dancing, running, yoga, swimming, and martial arts are some great options to try. Regardless of what type of mood you're in, if you move your body in a conscious way it will allow those feelings to pass through you with ease.

Principle 3: Fear Doesn't Have to Be So Scary!

We all know how debilitating fear can be, but it doesn't have to rule your life. We've found that if we're able to make friends with fear, accept that these types of feelings do come up at times, and then let them go with ease, we spend more of our lives feeling good, safe, and free. The opposite of fear is faith, and we've found that choosing the latter is far more empowering. So try out these exercises that will help you stand up to your fears in the most loving way possible.

Practice: The Fear Pot

This is a great way to recognize what your biggest fears are and then let go of them and the control that they have on your life. The first step is to take a blank piece of paper and write down your top five fears—the ones that are holding you back the most from your ideal life. While it may be challenging just to write these down, we ask that you trust the process—after all, awareness is the all-important first step.

The next step is to take each of these five fears and write each one out on a separate piece of paper. Once this is done, find a garbage can. Then read each of the fears out loud to yourself, inhale deeply, and as you let the breath out, begin to rip the fear up into pieces. Throw away what remains of that fear. Once this is completed, say out loud: "This fear no longer controls me; I choose faith and love instead." Repeat this process with each fear.

Just ripping up the pieces of paper is a great release, and this process can be incredibly therapeutic. The reason for the garbage can is that this is where your fears belong—with all the other trash you dispose of.

Practice: Fear-Thought Substitution

Take out a blank piece of paper. Create a column called "Fear Thoughts." Under this, begin by writing down all of the fear thoughts that pop into your head.

Then create a second column called "Faith Thoughts." Now take each of your fear thoughts and create a corresponding faith thought. We want you to get in the habit of training your mind to substitute fear with faith every time it comes up. The more you practice this process, the easier it will be. Eventually, you'll train your unconscious mind to focus on faith instead of fear.

Here are some examples to get you going:

Fear Thoughts	Faith Thoughts
I'm never going to meet this deadline.	I have everything I need to finish with plenty of time to spare.
What if I'm really sick?	I am well, and I embrace all that life brings me with an open mind.
My boss will never give me a raise.	I'm worthy of a raise, and I'll ask for one with confidence.
I'll never get that job I want.	There are lots of great jobs out there, and I know I'll get one.
I'll never meet the right person to marry.	The world is full of wonderful people I could fall in love with.
I'll never be rich.	I'm intelligent and resourceful, and I'll always have enough money.

Practice: Daily Gratitude List

We've found that gratitude is a great thing to focus on when we're feeling afraid.

Instead of thinking about all the things that aren't going to work out in your life, begin to concentrate on what's going well—right now! To do this, create a daily gratitude list. At the beginning and/or end of each day, spend some time writing down all the things that you can think of that you're grateful for. It can begin with something as simple as, "I am grateful to have all five senses," or "I am grateful to have a roof over my head, clothes to wear, and food to eat." This may feel challenging at first, but don't worry, that's normal.

If you've spent most of your life occupied with what you don't have or what you're afraid of, then it can be difficult to shift to being grateful for everything. Whenever you feel fear or panic come up, pull out your gratitude list and read it. This will allow you to shift your focus and, as a result, change how you're feeling.

Principle 4: Take Responsibility for Your Own Life

Being personally responsible means that you recognize that only you have the power to change your life. In order become personally responsible, you'll first need to understand yourself better. The better you know yourself, the less likely you are to be irritated or upset by others. Only you have the power to make yourself happy or sad.

Practice: Mirror, Mirror on the Wall

Have you ever found yourself in a situation where someone said or did something to you and you totally freaked out? Afterward, you may have been surprised by your own reaction, not knowing where it came from. When another person's words or actions bother you, the best way to deal with or understand it is to remove him or her from the situation.

It is in the act of removing all personal associations that we allow ourselves to get to the heart of the matter, which is the behavior. We believe that what we feel (when someone says or does something to us) has very little to do with the individual who's doing that thing to us, and more with the behavior he or she exhibits.

Example: Let's assume that your boss barges into your office and orders you to submit a document to him by the end of the day. You instantly feel your blood start to boil. Anger rises within you. You'd love to tell him where to go—but you respond to his demands politely instead. He leaves, and you're furious and resentful.

Step One: First, remove your boss, all associations with him, and his previous behaviors from this equation. Now, hone in on the behavior he's demonstrating that's truly bothering you. Look at the action and the words that are agitating you most. Let's say you *hate being ordered to do anything.* You don't like how *impolite* your boss is or how *ungrateful* he is for the hard work you do.

Once you can identify the behavior, you know that this, on some level, is what you're resisting. Maybe you're an extremely polite person, but you have trouble managing your own team because you're afraid to offend anyone or ask too much of them. Maybe this is because, as a child, your parents and teachers taught you that being polite is extremely important and that you must never speak rudely to anyone. You overcompensate by being too amiable but hate yourself for it, because you're never able to speak your mind in fear of insulting someone.

At this point, it's helpful to look within and see this behavior at work in your own life. You'll most likely notice that when you express the same characteristics, you feel some resistance that creates friction. When you do ask your team or your kids to do something, you tiptoe around it and end up doing the task yourself most of the time. This leaves you feeling taken advantage of and resentful.

Step Two: Since all behaviors have both a negative and positive side, try taking this one and find a way that it can serve a positive purpose.

Now, this may not come right away, and it often helps to have someone practice this with you who's gentle and kind and won't push any other buttons in the process.

Ordering someone to do something might be similar to *being assertive,* which can help you get things done and stand up for yourself. This is a quality that may actually have some merit when it comes to managing a team or a family. If you can begin to see this attitude in a new light, you can begin to embrace the fact that you, too, possess it within yourself.

If you accept what it is that bothers you so much about this behavior, it will no longer upset you nearly as much. Once you make peace with it and your own related struggles, observe your reaction the next time you witness it in other people. No longer will you take the demands of your boss so personally. You'll understand that he is just trying to get things done and is probably feeling pressure to report to his boss in a timely manner. Maybe he has trouble being assertive, so he overcompensates by sounding rude or unappreciative. It may not really be about you at all.

Principle 5: Be the Authentic You

Getting to know your true self takes time and practice. Everyone has an authentic self, but sometimes it's buried deep within, under the expectations and beliefs that others have heaped upon you.

We can tell you from experience that there's no better feeling than living from your place of authenticity and being true to yourself 100 percent of the time. On occasion, you may think you're being authentic, only to find out that a particular characteristic or behavior isn't actually yours and was likely handed down from a parent or elder and adopted unconsciously. To uncover your true self, you'll need to spend some time getting to know yourself. These exercises will help you set out on the journey of living the *authentic you!*

Practice: Getting to Know Your True Self

Step One: The first step is to identify all of the character traits that you feel represent who you are. One way to do this is to write the phrase, "If you really knew me, you would know that I am . . ." and then list all of the answers you think describe you. Be honest with yourself, as the deeper you go the more truth you'll reveal. This may take more than one try, so keep adding to this list each time. Here is an example:

If you really knew me, you would know that I am . . . kind to others.

If you really knew me, you would know that I am . . . compassionate.

If you really knew me, you would know that I am . . . empathetic.

If you really knew me, you would know that I am . . . hard on myself.

If you really knew me, you would know that I am . . . a perfectionist.

If you really knew me, you would know that I am . . . a worrier.

If you really knew me, you would know that I am . . . intuitive.

If you really knew me, you would know that I am . . . disorganized.

Step Two: From the list you've just created, go through each characteristic and classify whether it feels good or not. Take some time to reflect on your emotions when you're exhibiting this attribute. There's no hurry to do this part of the practice, since the more time you take to observe how you feel when you are experiencing these behaviors, the more accurate the image of your true self will be.

Sometimes you'll think that you feel good about a particular attribute, but upon closer examination you realize that this isn't really the case. If a character trait that you possess doesn't make you feel good, this is a solid indication that in some way it isn't part of your authentic self. The more comfortable you feel about an attribute, the more it is a part of your authentic self.

Let's continue with the example from above—evaluating each characteristic and going as deeply as possible to examine the feelings it brings up. Here's how this step might be written out. You can use our phrases in italics to prompt deeper responses.

If you really knew me, you would know that I am . . . disorganized.

First response: "This feels good, because people who are organized are totally controlling, and I'd rather be messy and disorganized so that I'm free to be creative and spontaneous."

Upon closer examination: "This might not always feel good, since sometimes being so disorganized means I'm late or unprepared, and my work suffers as a result."

Going even deeper: "Come to think of it, being disorganized is causing me more stress than it's worth, because I'm always running around looking for things I've lost, running late for meetings, having to apologize, and so on."

Is <u>disorganized</u> my authentic character trait? "Probably not."

Step Three: As we explained in Chapter Three, all behavior traits exist on a continuum. To help identify your authentic self, we need you to determine the polar opposite of each attribute that you don't feel good about.

Example
If you really knew me, you would know that I am . . . disorganized.
Polar opposite: organized.

Now, for the next three days allow yourself to behave a bit more toward the opposite trait. The object is to find a place where you feel totally comfortable and at ease, somewhere between your current point and the other end of the spectrum. This will be your authentic spot on the continuum for this particular behavior. Remember to practice the process with each trait that you've listed. The more you do, and then find your comfort zone on the continuum for each one, the more you'll be living from your authentic self.

Working with our examples, the spectrum would look like this:

Disorganized---------x----------xx---------xxx----------**Organized**

This is what a sample practice might look like:

Day one: x

Today I'll try to be a bit more organized by making a list of all the tasks I need to complete and checking them off as I go. I'll also leave space for flexibility, should anything unexpected come up.

Day two: xx

Today I'll try being even more organized. I'll clean my office, throw out all the clutter, and organize my day on a schedule and force myself to stick to it.

Day three: xxx

Today I'm going to behave as an extremely organized person would. I'll plan my schedule out, hour by hour, and check things off as I complete them; keep my work space completely clear of clutter; plan ahead by making schedules for the upcoming week; and organize my personal life as well, preparing menu plans and timetables for my kids.

Analysis

By doing this exercise, I realize that extreme organization is truthfully not my thing. I enjoyed the structure that I put in place; however, I definitely cannot operate as a totally organized person would. My comfort zone is probably around x, where I'm free to be flexible yet in control of my day to some extent.

Once you've gone through the process and determined where your authentic self sits on the spectrum, consider renaming the character trait above that did not feel good to you. Can you come up with a title that feels better and more genuine to your personality?

Authentic self: If you really knew me, you would know that I am . . . flexible and spontaneous with just enough structure to be productive.

Principle 5: Make Your Beliefs Your Own

Now that you've finished reading this book, we hope it has made you question some of your current beliefs and examine them to determine if they're serving you well or not.

We both had to excavate a lot of old beliefs and replace them with new ones in order to be true to ourselves and live in an empowered way. Some of them are so deeply rooted that it's hard to dig them up. This next exercise will serve as your shovel!

Practice: Out with the Old, In with the New

Step One: Question All Your Current Beliefs

Think back to when you were growing up and reflect on all the things that you were taught by your parents, siblings, teachers, and so on. These should pop into your mind quite easily, because they were ingrained into your consciousness at an early age. They have most likely become things that you believe to be the truth today. Here are some possibilities:

- You must work hard to get ahead.
- You won't succeed in life without an education.
- Be respectful of your elders.
- Beauty is on the inside.
- It's important that others like you.
- Expressing emotion is bad.
- Be true to yourself.
- Save the best for last.
- Don't get too excited, or you'll be disappointed.
- Help those in need.
- You must earn a lot of money to be successful.
- It's important to have fun in life.
- Live each day as if it's your last.

Some of these may seem ridiculous when put down on paper, but somewhere in your subconscious you still believe them to be true. Others you may have already let go of, and others still are more valuable now than ever before. Once you've completed your list, start questioning each of these beliefs: *Is this still my truth? How does it make me feel?* Ask yourself probing questions to determine whether they're all truly your own or if they belong to someone else. This will help you determine which ones you want to keep around and which ones you want to replace. Here are some more questions to begin with:

- Do I really believe this, or is it something that I've just been taught to believe as the truth?
- Does this even make sense?
- How does this belief make me feel?
- Does this belief scare me?

Try to be completely honest with yourself when you answer these questions, and record your answers as they come up.

Step Two: Substitute New "Feel Good" Beliefs

For all of the beliefs above that you identified as no longer making sense, no longer holding truth, or no longer making you feel good, it's time to find replacements that feel better. Here are a few examples to get you started:

Old belief: Expressing emotion is bad.
New belief: It's important and empowering to express my emotions in a healthy way.

Old belief: Money makes me successful.
New belief: My success is determined by many things—most important, how I feel about myself.

Old belief: Save the best for last.

New belief: As I enjoy all the good things in life, more good things will come to me.

Principle 6: Tap into Your Intuition—
Your Internal-Guidance System

We all possess an internal-guidance system called *intuition* or *sixth sense* or *gut feeling,* and this can come in handy when you're trying to make an important decision. If you listen closely, you'll hear your gut speaking loud and clear, telling you what to do. It won't be scary or overbearing, but more like a nudge in the right direction. These exercises will help you tune in to and tune up your intuition!

Practice: Be Spontaneous

Spontaneity is a powerful practice to get you in the habit of relying more on your instincts without overanalyzing a situation. It's about acting on a whim and making a quick, in-the-moment decision without much planning.

We believe that spontaneity is based more on your feelings, while planning is based more on your thoughts. Because intuition is also more about feeling, the more you practice being spontaneous, the easier it will be to connect to and trust your intuition. Here's what you need to do: for the next week, try to be spontaneous at least once a day. This may seem difficult for some and easy for others. If this is easy, challenge yourself to do it three to five times a day.

Here are some examples of spontaneous actions:

- Go for a walk without deciding ahead of time where you're going. Instead of mapping your route out in your head, just walk and let your feet guide you.

- Go out to eat somewhere new, and order the first thing on the menu that draws your attention.

- Plan an impromptu getaway with very little structure. Book a flight, get in your car and just drive, or take a vacation in your own city. Whatever you do, go with the flow as much as possible.

Smaller and less-dramatic spontaneous actions include:

- Pick up the phone and call someone as soon as he or she pops into your head.

- Get up and dance around your office as soon as you feel the urge.

- Go into a bookshop and buy the first book that you're drawn to without reading the back cover or even opening it.

- The next time you're driving by a store that catches your eye, park your car and go in.

- When you see a person who looks familiar or interesting, strike up a conversation.

You'll notice that if you aren't used to practicing this, it can be difficult at first, yet very invigorating at the same time. You may even find doors opening for experiences you never thought possible. Be gentle with yourself throughout the process. As you practice, you'll not only build up the ability to be more spontaneous but also more intuitive as well. Continue onward with a daily spontaneity practice at a pace that feels good to you.

Practice: Unleash Your Creativity

This practice will help you get more in touch with your creative side.

Step One: If you don't consider yourself a creative person, spend the next week taking part in any form of creative expression at least three times. This can be anything from drawing to dancing, singing, acting, painting, designing, writing, or taking photographs. The possibilities are endless. Even if this doesn't come naturally at first, try to get in touch with your inner artist. It may be buried deep, but know that it's in there. No matter what, don't judge your abilities when doing this practice. Even if you're just doodling, splashing paint on a canvas, dancing around your living room, or singing in the shower, it's fine, because this creative expression is for you alone.

Step Two: For those of you who already have regular creative practices in your lives, jump to this step.

Now we want you to practice creativity intuitively. If you chose to draw or paint, try doing your next piece without any plan at all. Put your marker or brush to the paper, close your eyes, and let your instinct guide you through each line or stroke. If you like to act, try doing some improvisation. If you sing or dance, then try freestyle or make up your next moves or song on the spot. The idea is to ditch the script and let your intuition flow. Because you have opened up your creative side already, this will be easier to do, and thus will strengthen your intuition very effectively.

ACKNOWLEDGMENTS

This book has been an incredible opportunity for both of us that wouldn't have been possible without the amazing people in our lives who have helped and supported us both personally and professionally. Although we're blessed to have such an incredible group of family and friends, there are far too many to name everyone here. Thanks to you all for your inspiration, guidance, positive energy, and supportive vibes.

We would like to thank personally those who had a direct impact on the writing, editing, and creating of this project.

To Hailey Eisen (**www.haileyeisen.com**), our editor, sister, daughter, and collaborator: your creativity, talent for transforming our concepts and ideas into beautiful prose, patience, and eye for detail all contributed to making this book a success. Although you took on the role of editor, your hand in this book went beyond that, helping us to tell our stories and share our messages in a more powerful and impactful way. We are lucky to have someone with your skills and talent in our family, because your closeness to the story meant you were able to truly understand where we were coming from and help us express it in a clearer and more authentic way.

To Lois Eisen, our wife, mother, and unofficial proofreader, thank you for your unwavering support, not only throughout the entire process of contemplating, writing, and editing this book, but also throughout our lives. You kept our family together through difficult times, ensured there were always good times, and helped us see the good in each other. This book literally would not exist if it weren't for your patience, kindness, commitment, and love. Thanks for always believing in this book and in our ability to share our message with the world. Thanks for inspiring us and standing by us, no matter what.

To Louise Hay, whose belief in us, our message, and our purpose to inspire and empower the next generation made all of this possible. Thank you for the insightful guidance, assuring support, and compassionate love that you provided throughout the whole process. We are so grateful for the eloquent and thoughtful Foreword that you wrote, and we cannot thank you enough for all that you have done to help us share our message with the world!

To Reid Tracy, president and CEO of Hay House, thank you for opening the door to the Hay House family and welcoming us in with warmth and kindness. We can't think of a better new family to be a part of. Thank you for taking a chance on us, our message, and this book. We are so grateful for all the support and mentorship that you have provided along the way and your commitment to working with us to reach a younger audience.

To Shannon Littrell, managing editor of Hay House, whose patience, heartfelt kindness, and true understanding made this whole process easier and more joyful, thank you for always responding quickly to our questions with such warmth. Thank you for sharing in our passion for this book, as we truly felt understood throughout. Thank you for making the experience of our first book a truly memorable one. It was such a pleasure to work with you!

ABOUT THE AUTHORS

Jeffrey Eisen

After more than 30 years of successfully growing and managing a multimillion dollar steel distribution and fabrication business as president and CEO, Jeffrey Eisen left the corporate world to embark on an intense journey of self-discovery. He realized, at the age of 50, that he cared more about people than profits and wanted nothing more than to dedicate his life to awakening, empowering, and inspiring others by sharing his love and wisdom. Since giving up his active role in the business, Jeffrey has become a life coach, spiritual guide, inspirational speaker, and writer. As a coach, Jeffrey focuses on experiential learning rather that just theory. He is committed to "walking the talk" in every aspect of his life and coaches by example. He lives his passion every day, working to help people find true happiness, contentment, and inner peace.

Jeffrey's other passions include photography and travel. He loves capturing the magnificent beauty of nature from around the globe and sharing it on his photo website **www.jeffreyeisen.com**. He lives in Toronto, Canada, with his wife, Lois, and has three children and two grandchildren. To learn more about Jeffrey's coaching practice and gain access to a wealth of inspiring resources, please visit **www.awakeningtheself.com.**

Michael Eisen

Michael Eisen is the founder of the Youth Wellness Network (YWN), an organization dedicated to inspiring and empowering youth across the globe to live happier and more positive lives. YWN specializes in creating and implementing wellness programs in schools and organizations, while providing additional assistance online through their ambassador training program (**www .ywnambassadors.com**). Michael is also a passionate, authentic, and charismatic speaker, author, and social entrepreneur.

After positively transforming his own life at the age of 19 and overcoming challenges with stress, anxiety, depression, and sickness, he is now driven to share with other young people the principles, strategies, and practices that empowered him to start living a happier and healthier life. Michael's struggles as a child impacted his life in such an intense way that they've inspired his lifelong crusade to help youth avoid living through the trauma he experienced.

Michael created YWN at the age of 25 in order to provide youth with more access to extensive support programs and resources that are specifically designed to create sustainable solutions to their most pressing issues and challenges. He offers a fresh, young, and authentic voice to the field of wellness and is rapidly becoming known as a youth-wellness expert. Michael lives in Toronto, Canada.

To learn more about Michael, please visit **www.michaeleisen .ca**, and to learn more about the Youth Wellness Network, please visit **www.youthwellnessnetwork.ca.**

NOTES

NOTES

NOTES

NOTES

NOTES

NOTES

NOTES

NOTES

NOTES

NOTES

We hope you enjoyed this Hay House book. If you'd like to receive our online catalog featuring additional information on Hay House books and products, or if you'd like to find out more about the Hay Foundation, please contact:

Hay House, Inc., P.O. Box 5100, Carlsbad, CA 92018-5100
(760) 431-7695 or (800) 654-5126
(760) 431-6948 (fax) or (800) 650-5115 (fax)
www.hayhouse.com® • **www.hayfoundation.org**

Published and distributed in Australia by: Hay House Australia Pty. Ltd.,
18/36 Ralph St., Alexandria NSW 2015 • *Phone:* 612-9669-4299
Fax: 612-9669-4144 • www.hayhouse.com.au

Published and distributed in the United Kingdom by: Hay House UK, Ltd.,
292B Kensal Rd., London W10 5BE • *Phone:* 44-20-8962-1230
Fax: 44-20-8962-1239 • www.hayhouse.co.uk

Published and distributed in the Republic of South Africa by: Hay House SA
(Pty), Ltd., P.O. Box 990, Witkoppen 2068 • *Phone/Fax:* 27-11-467-8904
www.hayhouse.co.za

Published in India by: Hay House Publishers India, Muskaan Complex,
Plot No. 3, B-2, Vasant Kunj, New Delhi 110 070 • *Phone:* 91-11-4176-1620
Fax: 91-11-4176-1630 • www.hayhouse.co.in

Distributed in Canada by: Raincoast, 9050 Shaughnessy St.,
Vancouver, B.C. V6P 6E5 •
Phone: (604) 323-7100 • *Fax:* (604) 323-2600 • www.raincoast.com

Take Your Soul on a Vacation

Visit **www.HealYourLife.com®** to regroup, recharge, and reconnect with your own magnificence. Featuring blogs, mind-body-spirit news, and life-changing wisdom from Louise Hay and friends.

Visit **www.HealYourLife.com** today!

CPSIA information can be obtained
at www.ICGtesting.com
Printed in the USA
FSOW01n1829140917
38685FS